After a California Earthquake

University of Chicago Geography Research Paper no. 233

Series Editors

Michael P. Conzen
Chauncy D. Harris
Neil Harris
Marvin W. Mikesell
Gerald D. Suttles

Titles published in the Geography Research Paper series up to no. 232 are now distributed by the University of Chicago Press.

After a California Earthquake

Attitude and Behavior Change

Risa Palm and Michael E. Hodgson

The University of Chicago Press
Chicago and London

Risa Palm is professor of geography and dean of the
College of Arts and Sciences at the University of Oregon.
Michael E. Hodgson is assistant professor of geography at
the University of Colorado, Boulder.

The University of Chicago Press, Chicago 60637
The University of Chicago Press, Ltd., London
© 1992 by The University of Chicago
All rights reserved. Published 1992
Printed in the United States of America
00 99 98 97 96 95 94 93 92   5 4 3 2 1

Library of Congress Cataloging-in-Publication Data

Palm, Risa.
        After a California earthquake : attitude and behavior
    change / Risa Palm and Michael Hodgson.
            p.   cm. — (University of Chicago geography research
    paper : no. 233)
        Includes bibliographical references and index.
        ISBN 0-226-64499-5 (pbk.)
        1. Insurance, Earthquake—California. 2. Earthquakes—
    Economic aspects—California. 3. Homeowners—California—
    Attitudes. 4. Earthquakes—Public opinion. 5. Public
    opinion—California.
    I. Hodgson, Michael E. II. Title. III. Series.
    HG9981.P35   1992
    368.1'22—dc20   91-857
                                                                          CIP

Contents

Figures

Tables

Acknowledgments

This monograph is based upon work supported by the National Science Foundation under grant no. BCS-9003573. The 1989 survey referred to in the text was supported by the National Science Foundation under grant nos. BCS-8802896 and BCS-8943381. Any opinions, findings, and conclusions or recommendations expressed in this material are those of the authors and do not necessarily reflect the views of the National Science Foundation.

The research assistants who worked on this project were R. Denise Blanchard and Donald Lyons. Denise and Don acted as a team in assisting with every part of the project, from the design of the survey instrument through the execution of the Dillman survey, the compilation of findings, and the development of statistical tests.

Secretarial assistance for the survey and the logistics of the research was provided by Regina Hanson. Patricia Peterson provided an outstanding contribution in copyediting the manuscript. Rachel Jarvis did editing and manuscript preparation.

We wish to thank Michael Conzen of the Geography Research Papers series and Penny Kaiserlian of the University of Chicago Press. We appreciate the helpful comments in the manuscript reviews by Howard Kunreuther and an anonymous reviewer.

The 1989 survey, on which some of the conclusions were based, was assisted by an advisory committee. Members of this committee were: Anne Butler, David Brookshire, James Brown, Sheldon Davidow, Harold T. Duryee, Walter Hayes, E. V. Leyendecker, Howard Kunreuther, Eugene LeComte, Edward Levy, Joanne Nigg, Sherry Oaks, and Richard Roth. Howard Kunreuther was very helpful and made many suggestions on both the ques-

xii ACKNOWLEDGMENTS

tionnaire and survey methods. Jack Evernden graciously lent us the original shaking intensity maps on which the risk analysis for San Bernardino and Los Angeles counties was based. Richard Roth has been an important contributor to this project, and served enthusiastically on the advisory committee. Bill Riebsame provided us with advice and encouragement throughout. David Morton was very helpful in identifying fugitive literature related to the project. We also thank Alex Goetz at the Center for the Study of Earth from Space for the use of his laboratory. As always, we wish to thank Bill Anderson of the National Science Foundation for his continuing intellectual guidance, support, and very helpful advice.

1

Earthquake Hazards and Preparedness

California—the state with the most rapidly growing population in the nation—is said to embody the American Dream. In California, a disaster is waiting to happen. Although most California residents know that the state is vulnerable to earthquakes, many persist in their lack of preparedness. Does experience with a moderate-scale earthquake jar people into action? Does such experience make them feel more vulnerable and therefore motivate them to take action? This issue, the impact of experience with an earthquake on attitude and behavior, is the subject of this monograph.

Despite the loss of life and property associated with damaging twentieth-century earthquakes, despite heavily funded campaigns to increase public awareness of the earthquake hazard and the measures available to protect life and property, and despite the concern of state and federal opinion-leaders for increasing awareness and preparedness, California residents continue to adopt voluntary hazard mitigation measures at a relatively low rate. Survey after survey has shown that fewer than 50 percent of California homeowners have insurance against earthquake damage other than the small policy mandated by the state (Palm et al. 1990, Roth 1990, Kunreuther 1990). Survey after survey has shown that few California residents adopt other mitigation measures, such as storing emergency supplies or developing a family emergency plan (Palm et al. 1990; Turner et al. 1979; Mileti, Farhar, and Fitzpatrick 1990, 1058-60). Finally, the development of state and local building codes and land use regulations that would reduce hazard vulnerability is slowed or impeded by local and state political and economic interests (Dames and Moore 1990, 4-16, 4-18).

But what about people who suffer property loss or read the barrage of publicity in local newspapers following an earthquake? Are these people more aware of the hazard? And does this awareness lead them to purchase insurance or adopt other measures to mitigate against personal and family losses? The purpose of the research reported here was to examine the shifts in attitude and behavior that occurred following the Loma Prieta earthquake in California in October 1989. The research also examined the ways in which experience with an earthquake affects adoption of mitigation measures and perceptions of vulnerability to future earthquakes. This study, which follows from a 1989 survey (Palm et al. 1990), provides a longitudinal glimpse into attitudes and behaviors, as well as the impacts of experience on attitude and behavior change.

The study shows that, as expected, the greatest shift in both attitude and behavior took place in the two northern California study areas that had been most directly affected by the earthquake (fig. 1). However, although homeowners expressed increased concern about a future earthquake, the purchase of earthquake insurance coverage increased only slightly in all four counties after the Loma Prieta earthquake. In addition, few homeowners adopted other mitigation measures to protect their lives or their property from future damage. These findings suggest that voluntary insurance purchase is unlikely to be universally adopted in California unless there is some major change in the cost structure or unless some other changes in the cultural, economic, and social context take place.

The context of this research requires an understanding of the economic factors that affect households and communities because of the earthquake hazard, the types of mitigation measures available, and the previous rates of adoption of these measures. It also demands a review of the factors that may cause changes in behavior with respect to hazards and that may promote the adoption of voluntary mitigation measures.

Economic Exposure to Earthquake Risk

The value of the property at risk in California is astounding. When the losses to individual households are compounded for regions, the probable losses easily equal billions of dollars. A frequent question is, what would be the loss to residential dwellings resulting from the greatest probable maximum earthquake within a region?

Damage at a given site is a function of the size of the earthquake, the attenuation of seismic waves along the path between the epicenter of the earthquake and the site, and the geologic conditions at the site. Damage can be associated with ground rupture (the sudden fracturing of the earth surface), fault creep (the slow and gradual fracturing of the earth), ground failure (landslides or liquefaction), ground shaking, and tsunami, or massive sea waves that may follow an earthquake.

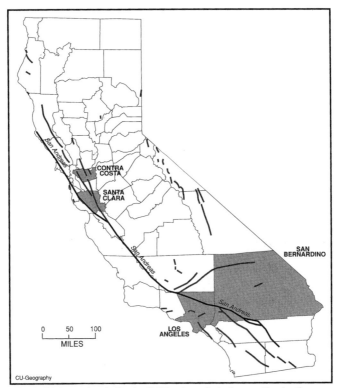

Fig. 1. *Major active faults in California and study counties in the pre– and post–Loma Prieta surveys.*

The vulnerability of buildings is a function not only of their location but also of their construction. Buildings constructed before 1940 are at greatest risk. Steinbrugge (1990) estimates that about 13 percent of all California structures are in this category. For example, Los Angeles contains 8,000 pre-1940 unreinforced masonry structures. Wood-frame houses withstand earthquakes well, but will fail if they are poorly constructed or if they have unbraced cripple walls, are not bolted to their foundations, or experience ground failure. Although many Californians live in structures meeting the post-1940 building standards, wood-frame homes constructed on alluvial soils are still at risk of damage, particularly if located where the water table is high.

A common calculation of the distribution of risk is known as the "probable maximum loss," or PML. The calculation of the PML requires information on (1) the spatial distribution of various kinds of dwellings exposed to ground shaking, landslides, liquefaction, and surface faulting associated with the earthquake; (2) the spatial distribution of these geologic hazards;

and (3) the susceptibility of each building type to loss from these hazards. The calculation methodology, which has been used for over twenty years (Steinbrugge et al. 1969, Algermissen et al. 1969), is still the most useful index of the distribution of probable loss.

In 1990, Steinbrugge (1990) reported on a set of PMLs to residential dwellings (1-4 unit dwellings) in various parts of California (table 1). Those areas with composite PMLs exceeding $10 billion include the Newport-Inglewood fault in Los Angeles and Orange counties, the Malibu-Raymond fault in Los Angeles County, the Whittier fault in Los Angeles County, the San Andreas fault in San Francisco and San Mateo counties, and the Hayward fault in Alameda and Santa Clara counties. These estimates are generated using a 8.25 M earthquake on the San Andreas fault and smaller magnitudes for the other faults.

Even these very large projections underestimate the total damage that would be caused by an earthquake, including the loss of jobs, the weakening of nationally important industry and defense facilities, the weakening of the banking system, and potential devastation of the insurance industry (Earthquake Project of the National Committee on Property Insurance 1989).

Table 1. Probable maximum losses (PML) to California 1-4 unit family dwellings in regions with known active faults

Southern California (Los Angeles and Orange counties area)	
Newport-Inglewood fault	$17.8 billion
Malibu-Raymond fault	12.0
Whittier fault	12.0
San Fernando fault	6.2
San Andreas fault	4.5
San Jacinto fault	2.7
Northern California (San Francisco Bay Area)	
San Andreas fault	14.7
Hayward fault	11.5
Calaveras fault	7.9
San Diego area	
Rose Canyon fault	3.5
Western regions of Riverside and San Bernardino counties	
San Andreas fault	2.5
San Jacinto fault	1.1
Santa Barbara area	
Arroyo Parida fault	0.7

Source: Steinbrugge 1990.

Mitigation Measures

What can individuals do to avoid some of the damage from a major earthquake? Many agencies, including the American Red Cross, the Department of Housing and Urban Development, the Federal Disaster Assistance Administration, the Governor's Office of Emergency Services, and the Federal Emergency Management Agency, and private corporations, have printed brochures on preparing for the emergency period of an earthquake. These preparations include planning how to locate family members after the earthquake; conducting practice drills; learning CPR and first aid; learning how to shut off gas, water, and electricity; securing the water heater, appliances, heavy furniture, heavy picture frames, mirrors, and air conditioners; storing flammable and hazardous liquids; and maintaining emergency supplies.

In addition, households can purchase earthquake insurance to protect against some of the financial losses following an earthquake. Insurance substitutes for, or at least supplements, disaster relief. It is available throughout the United States from private firms, and in addition, a small policy provided by the state is mandatory in California.

Indeed, homeowners may take many practical and inexpensive measures to prepare for the duration of an earthquake and its immediate aftermath. The adoption of some of these measures may save lives and reduce property damage.

The Adoption of Precautions

Many surveys indicate that the majority of California households do not prepare for earthquakes. A 1977 survey of 1,450 Los Angeles residents (Turner et al. 1980) showed that a large percentage of people living in an earthquake-prone area believe they cannot prepare for an earthquake— whether through the adoption of insurance or other measures. In response to the survey statement "There is nothing I can do about earthquakes, so I don't try to prepare for that kind of emergency," 41 percent agreed and, of these, 7 percent agreed "strongly." Almost one-third (32 percent) agreed with the even more fatalistic statement "The way I look at it, nothing is going to help if there were an earthquake" (Turner et al. 1980, 3).

Most of the respondents in the Turner et al. (1980) survey suggested actions that the government should undertake. The most frequent response was that the government should intensify public education (suggested by almost one-fourth of the respondents). Many respondents referred to efforts to upgrade the safety of structures, including the construction of earthquake-proof buildings, better enforcement of building codes, improvement of building codes, and the upgrading of old buildings. Others emphasized plans for emergency shelters and emergency medical care.

To assess whether residents were prepared as households or individuals for an earthquake and its immediate consequences, Turner and his colleagues asked homeowners to answer the following: "Please tell me if you have done any of these [suggestions of various agencies and groups concerned with earthquake preparedness] either because of a future earthquake or for some other reasons, whether you plan to do any of these things because of a future earthquake or for some other reasons, or whether you don't plan to do any of these." Ten of the listed activities were applicable for all households: having on hand a working flashlight, a working battery radio, a first-aid kit, and stored food and water; rearranging or securing cupboard contents and replacing cupboard latches; contacting neighbors for information; setting up neighborhood responsibility plans or attending neighborhood meetings. Other activities applied to families with young children: instructing children about what to do in an earthquake and planning emergency procedures for a reunion after the earthquake. Three other statements applied to owner-occupiers: whether they had inquired about earthquake insurance, bought earthquake insurance, or structurally reinforced their homes.

The authors concluded from the survey responses that "most households are unprepared for an earthquake and that the prospect of an earthquake has stimulated relatively little preparatory action" (p. 101). Although more than 70 percent had a working flashlight, and more than 50 percent had a working battery radio and first-aid kit, fewer than 30 percent stored food and fewer than 20 percent stored water or took any other precautions. Although 23 percent had inquired about earthquake insurance, fewer than 13 percent had bought it. Only about 11 percent had structurally reinforced homes. About half the families with young children had told them what to do in an earthquake, but fewer than 35 percent had set up emergency procedures in the residence, and fewer than 25 percent had plans for family reunion after an earthquake.

In 1979, Palm undertook a smaller survey of residents of Special Study Zones (surface fault rupture zones) in Berkeley and Contra Costa County to ascertain whether those who both received and recalled a disclosure that their property is within a Special Studies Zone would be more likely to adopt the same set of mitigation measures as the general population of Los Angeles (Palm 1981b). The study population was made up of recent home buyers who understood the meaning of a Special Studies Zone and were of higher average income and education than the general population. Although these residents were more likely to have inquired about earthquake insurance (41 percent), bought earthquake insurance (24 percent), and invested in structural reinforcements for their homes (9 percent), they were generally less likely than the Angelenos to adopt such mitigation measures as instructing children what to do in an earthquake, establishing emergency procedures at the residence, making plans for reunion after an earthquake, having a working battery radio, rearranging cupboard contents, contacting neighbors for information, or storing either food or water. Thus, studies completed in the late 1970s showed an astounding lack of individual or household preparedness.

More recent surveys in California show little change in this behavior. In a survey by the authors in 1989, fewer than 10 percent of the respondents answered affirmatively to the question "Have you done anything to minimize the amount of damage an earthquake might cause to your home?" Furthermore, even among the 10 percent who had undertaken mitigation measures, fewer than 50 percent had spent more than fifty dollars for such measures (Palm et al. 1990).

A last example is telling. Mileti and colleagues (1990) conducted a survey in Coalinga, Paso Robles, and Taft, California. These towns are within seventy-five miles of the predicted epicenter of a Parkfield earthquake forecast with a 90 percent probability between 1985 and 1993. If any individuals in any setting would be expected to undertake mitigation measures it would surely be these, since an earthquake was predicted as almost a certainty by the U.S. Geological Survey over a short time frame. In this study area, individuals were asked about preparedness actions they had taken since hearing the prediction of a Parkfield earthquake. Total percentage responses concerning preparedness are underestimated here, since some actions had been performed prior to the prediction. Yet in none of the communities surveyed and for none of the twenty-seven possible mitigation measures in the questionnaire did more than 31 percent of the respondents say that they had adopted that measure. The most frequently adopted preparedness actions in all three communities were to find out what to do during an earthquake (25-31 percent) and to stockpile emergency supplies (19-28 percent). Fewer took more expensive and time-consuming measures such as purchasing earthquake insurance (10-20 percent) or making the house more earthquake resistant (6-17 percent).

Judgment and Risk Behavior

Why do Californians resist the adoption of these mitigation measures? Does experience with an earthquake affect their behavior? One topic explored in this project is the relationship between changes in attitude and changes in behavior with respect to the earthquake hazard—the factors that promote or impede the adoption of voluntary mitigation measures. The topic of attitude formation and change, and the linkage between attitude change and behavior change, has been the subject of an immense amount of experimentation, particularly by psychologists and economists (for a review, see Weinstein 1989a). In general, assessment of risk is said to be affected by personal and social characteristics, the characteristics of the information or messages (how they are framed, how they are transmitted, and who transmits them), the experience of the individual or household with the hazard (whether direct and personal or vicarious), and location with respect to the risk—a surrogate for a number of variables including objective geophysical risk, perceived risk, and possibly experience with past disasters. We will examine these factors and their relationship to the research hypotheses in detail in chapter 4.

The empirical portion of this research addressed the relationship between changes in attitudes and in behavior at the individual or household level; however, behavior is highly constrained by factors other than attitude and opportunity. In a 1990 book, Palm argued that individual behavior is best understood within the context of the constraints and enablements set by the household, community, and society, including those arising from the political-economic system, cultural context, and media biases. For example, an individual may be highly aware of a hazard and the mitigation measures that would best address this hazard, but still be constrained from action by (1) powerlessness within the household; (2) lack of household resources to adopt the measures; (3) community or society mores discouraging adoption; (4) legal or bureaucratic impediments; or a host of other factors. Thus, we do not expect to see a direct and perfect relationship between attitude and behavior in the empirical world.

Constraints on the household or individual are set by the political-economic and cultural context, by resources, managers, and cultural assumptions. Given these constraints, how does the individual or household respond to hazards in the environment? The political economy and cultural values provide information to the individual and set constraints within which the individual can translate knowledge into effective action. The variability of responses arises from the translation of scientific knowledge about environmental risk into individual action. This process usually involves the individual's experience with the hazard and translation of the hazard into an element of life to be managed actively.

Awareness of the Hazard

Individuals vary in their awareness of the existence of local hazards. This awareness is in part a function of how long they have resided in the area and their personal experience with the local hazard condition. The seriousness of previous hazard events—the extent of loss of life and property damage—the recency of the event, and the extent of personal loss to the individual all have an impact on individual awareness.

Individual awareness can be enhanced by the amount of public information encountered by the individual, both from government agencies and from the general knowledge pool. Government agencies have attempted to increase the level of hazard awareness through a number of measures, including public information campaigns (warnings on inside covers of telephone books, community meetings, brochures), legislation requiring disclosure or insurance purchase, and dissemination of curriculum materials in the public schools. Information about the hazard may also simply be part of the general lore of the local area.

The nature of the physical environment itself may affect the amount of individual information. For example, when natural disasters occur frequently and regularly, households learn how to cope with the environmental variability.

Translation of Knowledge into Action

An individual's response to a hazard cannot be predicted solely by drawing conclusions about the amount of knowledge or experience he or she has with the hazard. Individuals must not only be aware of the existence of the hazard, but, before they will take action, they must also translate this knowledge into a belief that their own lives and property are susceptible to danger.

Many factors account for individual variability in the translation of knowledge into action. Although survey researchers tend to ask questions about age, income, sex, and educational levels of respondents, several studies have found that these demographic factors do not consistently affect either perception or response to hazards (Palm et al. 1990; Mileti, Farhar, and Fitzpatrick 1990; Drabek 1986).

However, five other factors do seem to be consistently related. First, the individual or household must have the resources available to adopt effective mitigation measures. The household must have the intellectual skills, the monetary resources, and the time to consider the hazard and possible mitigation measures, to select a set of measures, and to adopt them regardless of cost. Obviously such resources are unequally distributed in a population.

Second, individuals vary in the degree to which they believe that they control their own destiny or that it is controlled by others. Some researchers have suggested that this personality characteristic, known as "locus of control," relates in some way to the adoption of mitigation measures (Simpson-Housley and Bradshaw 1978). A related finding is that the pursuit of information itself and the adoption of some mitigation measure are likely to increase further self-protective behavior (Mileti, Farhar, and Fitzpatrick 1990). One might expect that those who believe they can affect their own circumstances are more likely to seek out information, and in that process, the problem and its solutions become more concrete to the individual. Mileti has termed this process "coming to 'own' the risk information" and argues that this is a primary factor mediating between acquiring information and taking action as a result of this information (1990, 1062).

Third, individuals personally calculate the probabilities that a given hazard will affect them, using all the decision-making heuristic errors suggested by psychologists. Their calculations may result in a perception of the likelihood of occurrence very different from that predicted by scientists studying the hazardous phenomenon, with concomitant behavior different from that predicted on a strict application of a utility model.

Fourth, the time frame used in decision making affects individual response. For example, an individual who feels committed to an area for a long period may be more likely to take into account hazards with low immediate probabilities but fairly high cumulative probabilities over time. In contrast, an individual who expects to live in an area for three years or less is very likely to ignore a low-probability risk with a high potential for damage.

Finally, a major factor affecting individual response to hazard is the salience of the hazard in comparison with other concerns. The individual will deal with natural hazards only when they seem more important than the other problems confronted in daily life.

Summary

California is highly vulnerable to losses of life and property associated with earthquakes. Yet recent studies show that few Californians are prepared to protect themselves from this serious problem in their environment. In the following chapters, we will revisit the 3,500 households surveyed in 1989 (Palm et al. 1990) to see the impact of the Loma Prieta earthquake on their outlooks and their adoption of mitigation measures. Since the mitigation measure most closely observed in the 1989 survey was the adoption of earthquake insurance, we will again focus on this response to earthquake vulnerability. Before describing the study, it is necessary to review the availability, cost, and regulation of earthquake insurance, as well as recent changes in its distribution resulting from changes in state legislation.

2

Earthquake Insurance

California property worth billions of dollars is susceptible to damage or loss from earthquakes. Homeowners can protect themselves from some of these losses by purchasing earthquake insurance. However, such insurance is held by a minority of California owner-occupiers. In this chapter, we will briefly review the nature and history of earthquake insurance and the factors that affect homeowner response to insurance.

The Nature and History of Earthquake Insurance

A popular notion is that earthquake insurance is too expensive or not available for the individual homeowner. Television and newspaper stories following the 1989 Loma Prieta earthquake commented on the problems of the uninsured. They noted that only 15 percent or at most 20 percent of the homeowners had insurance. Virtually all media accounts expressed surprise that so few homeowners in the region had earthquake insurance and attributed this lack of insurance to its high cost or unavailability. For people to elect to purchase earthquake insurance, they must know that it is available and decide that the cost of the premiums is not prohibitively high for the benefit of catastrophic coverage.

Earthquake insurance has been available since 1916 and may be purchased simply as an addendum to fire insurance policies. As mandated by state law, it is available from all companies that sell other homeowner's insurance in California at all times except for a short period immediately after an earthquake.

Costs of insurance include two components: the premiums paid by the insured and the deductibles. Premiums are the annual payments that must be made for a given amount of insurance (such as a premium of $2 for every

$1,000 of coverage). In this example, the annual premium on a house that was insured for $200,000 would be $400 per year. The second part of the cost is the deductible. The deductible is the portion of the loss that must be paid by the homeowners as their "share." A typical deductible in the case of earthquake insurance is 10 percent. This means that if a house insured for $200,000 suffers $50,000 in damage from an earthquake, the insurance company pays all but 10 percent of the insured value—or $20,000. In this example, the homeowner would pay $20,000 and the insurance company would pay $30,000. Premiums and deductibles are determined by the insurance rate zone in which the county of residence is located and the type of home construction. California includes three rate zones, with most of urban California in the zone with the greatest risk. Within a given zone, the least expensive premiums are paid by owners of small, wood-frame structures of three or fewer stories, since these homes have the most stable construction. The highest premiums are paid for unreinforced adobe, hollow clay tile, or unreinforced hollow concrete block buildings. In the highest-risk areas of California, coverage for wood-frame residential dwellings (the most common type of construction) costs about $2 to $2.50 per $1,000 of coverage with a 10 percent deductible. For example, the owner of a $300,000 property with $200,000 insurance on the house would pay an annual premium of $400 to $500. For this house, with a 10 percent deductible, the first $20,000 in loss to the structure would be deducted from any claim.

Disclosure of Availability

Recent California state legislation has promoted awareness of the availability of earthquake insurance. This legislation evolved from a set of legal interpretations protecting both the insurers and the insured (Brown 1987). The Superior Court of Marin County, California, in its *Garvey* decision, established the principle of concurrent causation: when two or more causes combine to produce a loss and when one of those causes is not excluded from insurance coverage, the loss is covered. This decision means that if an earthquake combined with poor construction causes structural damage, then damage from the earthquake is covered by the existing homeowner's policy.

As a result of extensive lobbying by the insurance industry, state legislation insulating insurance companies from this type of claim went into effect in January 1985. In exchange for protection from concurrent causation liability, the insurers had to offer homeowner's insurance policyholders the opportunity to buy earthquake insurance. The 1984 California legislation stated that "it is the intent of the Legislature in enacting this act to promote awareness of earthquake insurance by residential property owners and tenants by requiring insurers to offer that coverage" (§1081, sect. 2 of Stats. 1984, c. 916. California Insurance Code). Thus insurers in California are required to offer earthquake insurance as a condition for continuing to offer homeowner's insurance in this state.

In addition to specifying that insurers must offer earthquake insurance, the legislation states that an offer must be made by certified mail to demonstrate a "conclusive presumption" that it is voluntarily declined. The statute requires the insurance company's offer to contain the following language:

> Your policy does not provide coverage against the peril of earthquake. California law requires that earthquake coverage be offered to you at your option. The coverage, subject to policy provisions, may be purchased at additional cost on the following terms: (a) amount of the coverage: ____; (b) applicable deductible: ____; (c) rate or premium: ____. You must ask the company to add earthquake coverage within 30 days from the date of mailing of this notice or it shall be conclusively presumed that you have not accepted this offer. This coverage shall be effective on the day your acceptance of this offer is received by us.

This offer must be made prior to, concurrent with, or within sixty days following the issuance or renewal of a residential property insurance policy. Thus, the offer is renewed each time the policy is renewed.

The 1984 legislation was extremely important in making earthquake insurance widely available and in making this availability known to prospective purchasers. This legislation has ensured that information about the availability of earthquake insurance is provided to everyone who also carries homeowner's insurance. Clearly, the argument of unavailability is misplaced; people may choose not to buy earthquake insurance, but their decision is not related to its availability.

Potential Increased Purchase Rate

The insurance industry has not greeted the potential massive expansion of its market with great enthusiasm. Indeed, widespread purchase of earthquake insurance under current conditions could mean serious financial consequences for the industry.

The reasons for the industry problems are complex. The first issue is the actuarial computations—the definition of appropriate rates for the risks associated with earthquake hazards. Usually, insurance rates (premiums and deductibles) are set on the basis of experience, requiring the capacity to predict probabilities of particular losses over a regular period of time. Brown and Gerhart (1989) noted with respect to earthquake insurance that "the problem is that history has not yet provided a 'sufficiently large sample' nor has it been possible to dependably identify a 'sufficiently large number of exposure units' to permit effective application of probability theory." Thus, earthquake insurance cannot be considered under normal actuarial methods, compounding the problem of setting fair rates or calculating risks of collecting premiums and promising coverage.

Insurance company investment policy is also constrained by federal tax law. Companies could develop the capacity to cover the numerous claims possible following a major earthquake if an individual company or a coalition of companies collected a reserve pool. Federal tax laws, however, discourage the accumulation of large capital pools by treating them as taxable profits.

A third issue is the insurance industry claim that earthquake insurance is plagued by adverse selection, the tendency for only those at greatest risk to purchase the insurance. A basic principle of any insurance is that the risk is spread over a large population and that at any time only a small percentage of that population will actually suffer adverse economic consequences. In the case of earthquakes, companies argue: "Very few residential property owners and small businesses buy earthquake coverage. Additionally, . . . the individuals and firms that buy such insurance are usually located in seismically active areas. Hence, not only is the policyholder pool for earthquake coverage too small, but also the ones that buy earthquake insurance are the ones at the highest risk" (Earthquake Project 1989, 69). For these reasons, the industry argues that it is difficult to offer insurance at an affordable rate and spread the risk across a large and randomly distributed population base.

As a result of these serious concerns, the insurance companies have united to propose a cooperative arrangement with the federal government that would reduce their risk yet enable them to continue to provide earthquake insurance. The goal of this coalition is to pass federal legislation that would create a federal government/insurance industry partnership by setting up a Federal Earthquake Insurance and Reinsurance Corporation (FEIRC) to administer an earthquake insurance program. The Primary Residential Property Insurance Program would cover direct damage from an earthquake for residential property owners in states identified as at risk from earthquakes. Owners of residential property with mortgages backed or reinsured by a federal agency or issued by any federally insured institution would be required to purchase earthquake insurance. In addition, all insurers participating in the program would automatically include earthquake coverage in their insurance on residential property (Earthquake Project 1989). Enactment of such a program would provide security for the insurance industry against major catastrophic losses associated with large earthquakes.

Several versions of the proposed national earthquake insurance program were before Congress in 1991, differing primarily on the mandatory mitigation measures that communities and states would have to adopt as a condition of the insurance program (H.R. 4480 and H.R. 2806). According to a spokesperson of the Federal Emergency Management Agency (FEMA), the prerequisites of such a program would be: determination of the existence of and correction of market failure, actuarial fairness in rate structure, inclusion of hazard mitigation provisions to reduce the risk to life and property, federal oversight and control, deficit neutrality (that is, the program would eventually carry with it no deficits), and risk sharing by the private insurance industry (Kwiatkowski 1990). Specific state and community mitigation measures that might be associated with such a federal earthquake insurance program have been suggested in a study completed in 1990 (Dames and Moore 1990). As of summer 1991, none of the proposed congressional legislation had yet been adopted.

Insuring the Deductible

In the meantime, additional legislation at the state level has been passed that could affect the insurance setting: the California Residential Earthquake Recovery Fund was passed in 1990 and is expected to go into effect in early 1992. This legislation provides mandatory insurance of up to $15,000 in order to cover losses associated with the deductible on catastrophic insurance.

The legislation springs directly from experience with the Loma Prieta earthquake. This earthquake demonstrated to homeowners the impacts of a 10 percent deductible on their personal losses. As Roth (1990, 833) describes it, "Even though 30-35 percent of the homes had earthquake coverage, the deductible was 10 percent of the coverage, which often amounted to $20,000. A large number of people protested to their insurers and to the Legislature. People also protested over the 10 percent deductible after the Whittier earthquake." Although the industry had adopted a 10 percent deductible to reduce their risk in moderate earthquakes and therefore insure more homes with the same amount of capital, the 10 percent deductible became politically unsupportable. The result was pressure from homeowners for basic protection up to $15,000, a coverage that the insurance industry did not want to provide (Roth 1990, 833).

The new state program levies a surcharge of from $12 to $60 (depending on location and type of dwelling) on residential and mobile home insurance policies. These surcharges are collected by the insurance companies but sent to the California State Treasury to be placed in an account free of federal or state taxation. The program provides coverage up to $15,000 for the structure only, subject to deductibles of $1,000 to $3,500 (depending on the value of the house).

This new program drastically affects the individual householder's decision on supplemental earthquake insurance. A household with the means and motivation to attend to earthquake insurance will gather information relevant to the financial aspects of insurance purchase. The most significant information in the purchase decision would be the expected percentage of loss to the dwelling beyond the deductible, that is, beyond the amount that the insured policyholder would have to pay before the insurance company would pay for the remainder of the loss. Steinbrugge (1990) estimates that houses constructed before 1940 will suffer 2.3 times more loss than those built after 1940. About 13 percent of the housing in southern California consists of these older homes (Steinbrugge 1990, 805). Further, Steinbrugge estimates that few houses suffer more than 20 percent damage in the probable maximum intensity earthquake.

Before the new legislation, insured homeowners usually had to pay the first 10 percent (i.e., the deductible) of the insured value themselves, with the insurance company paying the balance. These proportions meant that, with a 10 percent deductible, a $40,000 loss on a $200,000 home (not unusual in the Loma Prieta earthquake) would cost the insured homeowner $20,000, with $20,000 paid by the insurance company. For a $100,000 loss, the insurance company would pay $80,000 while the homeowner paid the same $20,000.

The 1990 legislation mandated a small amount of earthquake insurance, and if this legislation goes into effect, the division of losses paid by the homeowner will change. For example, Steinbrugge suggests (table 2), that the owner of a $200,000 home (below the median home value in both Los Angeles and San Francisco) suffering a $40,000 loss would pay $6,000 and the State of California would pay $14,000. If the homeowner were insured, the insurance company would pay the remaining $20,000. For a 20 percent loss to a $500,000 insured home (an upper-middle-class home), the homeowner would pay $37,500, the state would pay $12,500, and the insurance company would pay $50,000. In contrast, the uninsured homeowner would pay $87,500, with the state paying $12,500. The homeowner might undertake these complex calculations in deciding upon a particular form of earthquake hazard mitigation—the purchase of an earthquake insurance policy.

At the time of the 1990 survey, the situation was simpler: the $15,000 maximum state policy was not available and owners had to decide between the extremes of insurance or no insurance. The new legislation will reduce the costs of small losses to homeowners; however, it does not address the risk of truly catastrophic losses. Indeed, the bill itself states, "The Legislature recognizes that the California Residential Earthquake Recovery Fund is not a substitute for the purchase of private insurance (Section 50121)," and Assistant Insurance Commissioner Richard Roth has testified to Congress that the California legislature "supports both private earthquake insurance and federal efforts" (Roth 1990, 833).

Thus, the homeowner's decision concerning earthquake insurance as a hazard mitigation measure remains the same after the 1990 California legisla-

Table 2. Loss borne by homeowner, State of California, and insurance company when homeowner also carried earthquake insurance with 10 percent deductible

| Value of home | Amount of loss | Losses paid by or borne by | | |
		Homeowner	State of California	Insurance company
$200,000	$20,000	$6,000	$14,000	$0
	40,000	6,000	14,000	20,000
	200,000	6,000	14,000	180,000
500,000	50,000	37,500	12,500	0
	100,000	37,500	12,500	50,000
	500,000	37,500	12,500	450,000

Source: Steinbrugge 1990.

tion: whether to pay an insurance premium to reduce the risk of a catastrophic loss.

Earthquake Insurance Purchase Decision

Insurance is available, disclosure of its availability is mandated by state law, and a small ($15,000) policy is now mandatory in California. Given this setting, how does the individual household evaluate the advantages and disadvantages of purchasing insurance for the damage not covered by the small state policy?

Since the empirical work reported here was completed before the new mandatory small policy went into effect, we must also ask, how do people decide on the purchase of any nonmandatory insurance? To answer this question, we refer to the framework developed by Palm (1990) within which environmental decision making should be cast.

Decision making at the household level is constrained by macroscale factors operating far beyond the individual: the cultural and institutional setting within which California households live.

The macroscale context for the insurance purchase decision includes the physical, political, and cultural environment. Not only is California "earthquake country," but this very phrase has become part of the state's image. The earthquake hazard does not surprise migrants to California, since it has been recognized from the time of earliest settlement. Inhabitants know that the region is underlain with many faults and that an earthquake on any of these, such as the one in the San Fernando Valley in 1971, the Whittier Narrows in 1987, or Loma Prieta in 1989, can cause deaths, injury, destruction of property, and disruption of life. This awareness of a dangerous physical setting should increase the propensity to purchase insurance, all else being equal.

Another aspect of the macroscale setting that is important for individual decision making is the cultural setting in California. In the state, a great deal of attention has been given to engineering or seismological efforts to mitigate the impacts of earthquake hazards, as opposed to individual or community nonstructural mitigation measures. This approach results partly from a cultural reliance on technology to solve problems, which tends to reduce individual responsibility and may place residents at even greater risk from major damaging earthquakes. For individual California homeowners, an assumption that technology can solve earthquake vulnerability may discourage self-protective behavior such as insurance purchase.

A related cultural characteristic is the shared value of individual as opposed to collective responsibility for general well-being. This emphasis on the individual household in U.S. society implies that the long-term consequences of the hazard fall on the individual household. Even though the community may recover from a natural disaster (Rossi et al. 1983), the household must rely on its own resources to find new housing and employment or to collect from an insurance company. This tendency should encourage insurance purchase.

Individual Behavior in Context

Before individuals are motivated to buy insurance, they must be aware of both the hazard and its implications for damage as well as the availability of insurance. State law requires insurance companies to provide information about the availability and cost of earthquake insurance. In addition, general information about earthquake hazards is disseminated by an increasingly large number of sources. Teacher training programs have been developed to introduce earthquake mitigation units into the public schools (Thier 1988). Scout organizations have earthquake mitigation badges. Local governments have sponsored earthquake awareness days; the most ostentatious, sponsored by the City of Los Angeles, involved especially developed footage of a simulated Los Angeles earthquake provided by Universal Studios (Mattingly 1988). Street atlases have overlays showing the surface fault rupture zones. Telephone books contain information on emergency procedures to follow during an earthquake. Real-estate agents are required to disclose location within a surface fault rupture zone. The U.S. Geological Survey, the Office of the State Geologist, FEMA, SCEPP, BAREPP, BICEPP, and other organizations provide brochures, maps, scientific papers, and other materials on the earthquake problem and the steps to mitigate some of its worst effects. The *Los Angeles Times* and other California newspapers have published maps and reports on earthquake hazards. In short, information about the distribution of fault traces or recommended steps to prepare for a major damaging earthquake is in the public domain. Such public information should increase the propensity to purchase insurance.

But awareness of the risk and of the availability of insurance is not a sufficient predictor of the insurance purchase decision. This decision is complicated by individual roles within the household, the household resources, beliefs about the efficacy of insurance as a means of protecting household assets, the relative salience of the earthquake hazard to household decision makers, and scores of other societal and political-economic factors. At the same time, many factors distort the individual's perceptions of the hazard as well as calculations of the costs and benefits of an action such as insurance purchase.

Summary

In this chapter, we have described the nature and history of earthquake insurance and recent state legislation that regulates its availability and cost. We have also explored some of the factors that affect individual response to insurance availability. In the next chapter we will describe the empirical setting of the study, focusing on the role of property in California and the integration of earthquake hazards into its assessment.

3

Property in California

Since the focus of this study is the protection of property through the purchase of insurance, it is important to understand the role of property—and especially homeownership—in California. House value and an emphasis on property ownership are essential components of the economic and cultural context in which California residents make an insurance decision.

In this chapter, we will focus on the nature of residential property. We will first consider two aspects of value associated with property, the symbolic value attached to owner-occupancy in American culture and the nominal or dollar value of the property. We will review the value attached to homeownership in American culture and then look at the way in which property market value has increased in California far beyond that in the rest of the nation. Finally, we will focus on the way the earthquake hazard is integrated into property value, whether in decisions to site facilities or housing units in hazardous areas or in the appraisal and mortgage loan activity that gives value to sites.

Nature of Residential Property

Symbolic Value of Homeownership

Homeownership has a significant symbolic value in American society (Palm 1981a). This value has had a marked effect on the internal structure of the city in the United States.

The ownership of land was one of the tenets of the very founding of this nation. Before the American Revolution, landownership brought with it the right to vote and an entire set of civil liberties and rights. After the Revolution, land law derived from English law was modified to guarantee that large tracts of land would not become the property of a limited number of families as it had in Europe and that land would be bought and sold according to the current economic market with few restrictions. These legal principles accompanied the notion that landownership was an integral part of citizenship in the new nation.

The value of homeownership has been integrated into national policy. The federal government has consistently emphasized the provision of owner-occupied housing by stimulating private enterprise. By providing tax incentives for households to borrow money to finance housing purchases, the government has encouraged debtor-financed ownership, enabling the financing of more single-family construction and providing profits to mortgage lenders and industries related to home construction.

Before 1932, there were few federal housing programs; those in existence were in the form of housing codes or state loans for construction. Several acts that went into effect in the 1930s revolutionized the federal approach to housing. In 1932, the Federal Home Loan Bank System was created to aid private mortgage lending institutions. Also in 1932, the National Housing Act established a Federal Housing Administration (FHA) to stimulate mortgage loans by insuring lenders against losses from borrower defaulting. In addition, the Federal Savings and Loan Insurance Corporation (FSLIC) provided federal insurance to individuals making deposits in savings and loan institutions, increasing the amount of capital available for home loans.

All of these practices remain in effect today, stimulating investment in the private housing market. An example of this continued preference of private over public housing, even for low-income families, was the 1968 Housing Act Section 235 program. This program permitted low-income families to buy homes with federal assistance. The family contracted to pay 10 percent of its income in monthly payments, while the federal government contributed the remainder. The program enabled low-income families to purchase single-family homes over a maximum mortgage period of forty years. Throughout this period the Internal Revenue Service code has allowed the deduction of home mortgage interest payments from taxable income, providing a major subsidy to owner-occupiers and encouraging this form of occupancy.

The symbolism surrounding homeownership has continued to the present. An owner (whether or not that person owns the property outright or is indebted to a mortgage lender) is seen as more stable and of better social status than a renter. As Marcuse has argued, "Ideologically, political as well as business leaders have long seen home ownership as buttressing stability, allegiance, thrift, hard work, and patriotism" (Marcuse 1990, 337). This ideology, which was a basis of national policy from the time of independence, supported policies making the acquisition of land inexpensive and relatively easy. At the turn of the century, housing reformers such as Lawrence Veiller were even more explicit about the link between homeownership and citizenship: "All observers agree that measured by the old standards, the apartment dweller shows a loosening of moral fiber. . . . [Homeownership] has great utility as automatically interesting the owner in government" (quoted in Marcuse 1990, 337).

Similarly, Franklin D. Roosevelt, in defending the then new Homeowners Loan Corporation, stated that "the broad interests of the nation require that special safeguards should be thrown around homeownership as a guarantee of social and economic stability" (quoted in Marcuse 1990, 337). But the home owned must also be in a particular neighborhood to achieve a certain level of social status. The status of neighborhoods is so important in American society that homeowners will pay more for a house located in a more prestigious neighborhood, even if the house construction value and all other services and amenities are held constant. For this reason, a house in Cherry Hills may sell for $50,000 more than the same model in Grassy Flats: neighborhood itself has taken on a status value in American society (Palm 1981a).

But homeownership has more than symbolic value. It also is a mode of financial investment for the middle class (Palm 1979). As England has been described as a "nation of shopkeepers," the United States can be considered a "nation of homeowners" in which individuals invest in their homes as capital goods (Perrin 1977). The combination of price inflation and continuing federal tax subsidy for mortgage interest has encouraged the use of housing as an investment (Johnston 1978).

Regarding a home as an investment helps explain the American concern for the exterior appearance of surrounding properties and the racial and economic composition of the neighborhood, since homogeneity of neighborhood contributes to the resale value of a house (Palm 1981a). In other words, a house is an investment, and its owner anticipates a profit from its resale; thus it is important that the character of surrounding property not detract from the value of the house.

Neighborhood homogeneity is valued in general ideology and therefore also in real-estate appraisal practice. Mixtures of multifamily housing with single-family houses, or mixtures of income, family style, or racial composition may threaten the selling price of the property by placing it within a "transitional" category (Beshers 1962, Berry 1976, Babcock 1968). Codes or covenants are often used to create and maintain neighborhood homogeneity. This treatment of neighborhood is a direct consequence of the cultural emphasis on private housing as a capital investment rather than simply as a mode of shelter.

Value of Property to Californians

While housing has an obvious value to its occupants—providing familiar comforts and shelter from the elements—property's more significant value is its exchange value, its monetary value on the market. This exchange value of housing has fluctuated wildly in recent years. Indeed, the value of a home became a standard conversation topic at cocktail parties in the late 1970s.

Throughout the 1970s California residents used housing as a speculative investment: "People here have been counting on their homes to build their fortunes" (*Time* 1982, 65). Many would-be owners engaged in creative financing, banking on price inflations to cover the very high costs of financing. One home financing plan involved the use of balloon payments, short-term loans against the property that became due in full within two to five years. Many borrowers who used this financing found that they could not pay off their loans or obtain new loans (*Time* 1982). Speculative lending practices in the 1970s, providing borrowers with second, third, or even fourth mortgages on property, resulted in increased foreclosure rates in the early 1980s as house prices stagnated. This speculation in California house prices contributed to the serious financial problems of the primary mortgage lenders—the savings and loan institutions—and eventually required the federal government to bail out savings and loan institutions in 1990.

Recent Inflation in Market Value

During the past twenty years, the emphasis on house value in California has been justified by a very rapid inflation in housing prices, with short pauses in the early 1980s and early 1990s. Overall, the pattern has been one of price escalation (fig. 2). The median house price in San Diego SMSA rose from $37,900 in 1973 to $171,000 in 1988; in the Los Angeles–Long Beach–Anaheim SCSA the median purchase price rose from $37,000 in 1973 to $187,300 in 1988, a 500 percent increase (Federal Home Loan Bank Board 1988). House prices in the San Francisco Bay Area rose even higher. Median purchase prices for houses in the San Francisco–Oakland–San Jose SCSA rose from $40,800 in 1973 to $201,100 in 1988, almost a 500 percent increase. In contrast, houses in Kansas City rose by 300 percent from $33,700 in 1973 to $108,700 in 1988; prices rose by about 280 percent in the Detroit–Ann Arbor SCSA from $35,700 in 1973 to $99,500 in 1988; and prices rose about 270 percent in the Milwaukee-Racine SCSA from $35,000 in 1973 to about $98,100 in 1988. The greatest increases in California house prices occurred during the 1980s; in a dramatic example, house prices more than doubled in San Diego between 1981 and 1988. Although the early 1990s saw a slowing of these increases, and in some cases a brief decline in house prices, the house price levels of California urban areas still remain far higher than those in other parts of the nation.

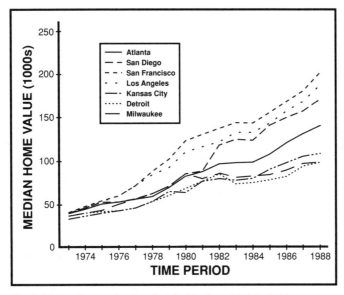

Fig. 2. Median home value in selected cities from 1973 to 1988.

The California house price increase is attributed to two factors: (1) a change in the nature of houses sold and (2) a simple inflation in the cost of existing housing. An example of the first factor is the construction of a new upper-price housing project dominating sales in a particular year and greatly increasing the median sales price. Although the first factor can play a role in a given year in a small area, the California housing market shows clear evidence of the impacts of the latter factor—sheer inflation in the sales price of housing.

Thus, housing not only has a symbolic value in American society, but also has been an effective investment in California in the past two decades. During the early 1990s this trend of rapid house price inflation has slowed, but housing and land remain a major component of household wealth in California. This factor makes the lurking presence of the earthquake hazard even more important. How does this hazard become integrated into the appraisal of land and the assignment of house prices?

Property Values

The change in the value of a home can be supported by the market only if it is backed up by real-estate appraisals and mortgage lenders. A market evaluation becomes a real value only when mortgage lenders provide 80-90 percent of the appraised value in a loan where the collateral is the house itself. During this process of appraisal and mortgage lending decisions we would expect to see the integration of environmental hazards into the expected sales price.

Land Valuation Models

In a previous book, Palm (1990) outlined the relationship between land valuation and environmental hazards. In a review of the various approaches to location theory that have evolved from economic geography, regional economics, and classical economics, Palm found that only scant attention has been paid to environmental factors in the analysis of location decision making. In most cases, the physical environment is considered a local factor, to be noted in a detailed site analysis only after making location decisions at a regional or intermetropolitan scale.

How then does the distribution of natural hazards affect the valuation of property and the decision to site particular facilities? Every location has both environmental amenities and environmental hazards. Indeed, when one points out to Californians that they live in earthquake country, they will invariably respond by pointing out the problems of hurricanes, tornadoes, or other hazards elsewhere. In a rational process, the environmental amenities and environmental hazards of each place would be assessed in the migration decision.

Despite the significance of environmental amenities and hazards in the migration or relocation decision, relatively little attention has been paid to this kind of trade-off in location theory research. In some cases, corporations or individual households have not previously been located in the areas to which they are considering relocating, and they are particularly uninformed about the full range of characteristics of these new environments. Although federal, state, and local governments have passed disclosure laws in house sales transactions, these laws have been spectacularly unsuccessful in providing appropriate information (Palm 1981b, Cross 1985). Thus, while decision makers ideally should be calculating rational trade-offs between amenities and drawbacks, the absence of systematic methods of informing new migrants about environmental hazards prevents such a process.

Much location theory has ignored the existence of natural hazards and focused only marginally on natural resources in explaining the location and relocation of human activity. Further, when environmental hazards are explicitly considered, their impacts on the decision process are complicated by the trade-offs between environmental risks and amenities, political factors that constrain location decisions, the time frames used by decision makers, and the availability of practical alternatives. The complications make it difficult to define clearly the impacts of environmental hazards on location decisions.

Natural Hazards in the Appraisal Process

Although the integration of hazards into the appraisal of property is not straightforward, a study of appraisal and lending practices would be expected to show some impact of earthquake hazards on property value. To focus on this issue, Palm et al. (1983) conducted empirical work on appraisal and lending practices.

Appraisals of a property are the key to its value. The market price estimate of a property determines the maximum mortgage loan from a lender, in turn influencing the price the seller can charge. How then are these appraisals done? Appraisers use three methods to assess the value of single-family residences: the market approach, the cost method, and the income approach. The market approach is the most common. By this method an appraiser estimates the probable price of a dwelling by looking at comparable properties sold in recent years and analyzing each comparable property with respect to date of sale, size of the property, features of the dwelling unit, location in the neighborhood, physical characteristics of the lot, and conditions of sale. The appraised price is not the same as the actual selling price (since the final price will be the result of negotiations between the seller and the buyer), but is an estimate used by lenders to decide the maximum home mortgage loan to be made available to the qualified buyer.

Appraisers are instructed to use particular criteria in estimating property value. Standard practice (Blankenship 1986, Bloom and Harrison 1978, Ratcliff 1965) involves the analysis of the improvements (e.g., dwelling units), the site (the lot), and the location of the neighborhood. Information on natural hazards could be integrated into the analysis of any of these factors. In assessing the house, the appraiser could seek information on visible damage from previous earthquakes and structural reinforcements that would make the dwelling more resistant to damage. In an assessment of the lot, the appraiser could check for susceptibility to landslides, liquefaction, or ground shaking. Similarly, the neighborhood could be checked for such factors.

Standard appraisal practice does not include specific directives on assessing factors relating to earthquake hazards. The Federal Housing Administration requires information on the visual appeal of the property, livability, natural light and ventilation, structural quality, resistance to the elements, and suitability of the mechanical equipment. Appraisers are instructed to provide descriptions of the house, site improvements, and the relationship of the house to the site. The lot description includes such factors as views, site improvements, hazards, and nuisances. One of the standard texts (Bloom and Harrison 1978, 1255) admonishes appraisers to investigate hazards, including "potential slides, earthquakes, dangerous ravines and bodies of water, or any unusual fire danger." Thus property appraisers may take note of such factors in their appraisal reports.

The final estimated value that appraisers report is based on probable market value—the selling price at a given time. Thus, while appraisers may report location on a floodplain or susceptibility to surface fault rupture, these factors do not play a clearly defined role in appraised values. For this reason, surveys of both appraisers and home mortgage lenders were undertaken in 1983 (Palm et al. 1983) to obtain opinions about the influence of earthquake hazards on assessments of home values.

In early 1983, thirty California appraisers were asked to describe the site characteristics most important to value, their clients' perceptions of the importance of hazardous site conditions, and any adjustment in price that would be made if a property were located in a floodplain or in a fault rupture zone (Palm et al. 1983). Few appraisers mentioned environmental hazards as affecting sales price, few felt that clients (lenders, buyers, and sellers) regarded such hazards as important in the sale price estimate, and few investigated the influence of these factors on comparable homes. When asked to estimate the current price of a standard home and the adjustment in this price for location in a surface fault rupture zone, most (75 percent) said there would be no price reduction. Only if structure damage from previous earth movement were evident would the price be reduced, although even then 40 percent said there would be no price adjustment. This study concluded that appraisers feel that environmental hazards cannot and should not be isolated from the many other variables that determine the value of a property, although they do feel that they have a professional responsibility to report their existence to their clients.

In the same study (Palm et al. 1983), home mortgage lenders were surveyed to determine the ways in which they integrate information from appraisers into lending decisions and the value they place on earthquake hazards in their decisions. In late 1982, thirty lenders in the Seattle region and ninety lenders in California were interviewed. The vast majority (76 percent in California) said they do not consider seismic risk when evaluating loans on residential property. All the lenders ranked a possible earthquake as the least significant of probable causes of mortgage default (after flood, fire, divorce, and unemployment). Few California lenders had made a loan modification (e.g., changing the down payment requirement, adding additional loan charges, or requiring earthquake insurance) because of location in a landslide-prone area or in a surface fault rupture zone, or even because of evidence of damage from seismic or other geologic activity.

Finally, the study of Palm and others (1983) included a statistical analysis on the probability that a loan would be granted in California in the 1979-80 period. Approximately 100,000 loan applications from ten California counties were analyzed; of these almost 10,000 were located in surface fault rupture zones (Special Studies Zones). The authors hypothesized that the decision to accept or reject a loan application would be related to the ratio of the sales price to borrower income, the age of the dwelling unit, whether it was to be owner-occupied or rented, the ethnicity of the borrower, and whether the property was located in a Special Studies Zone. During this period, about 88,500 of the applications were accepted and almost 10,000 denied.

Hedonic price analysis showed that for all counties, loans were more likely to be granted to non–African American borrowers, for housing that was newer and owner-occupied, and to borrowers whose incomes were relatively higher with respect to the sales price. Hispanic borrowers and locations within Special Studies Zones were not disadvantaged in the loan decisions. These relationships held at the county (submarket) level as well, with slight variability in the relationship between ethnicity and lending decision. Location in a Special Studies Zone was not statistically significantly related to the lending decision in any of the counties except Alameda and Riverside, where the sign of the relationship is reversed; that is, the property within the zones is more likely to receive a favorable decision than property outside the zones. In sum, location in a Special Studies Zone did not have a negative impact on the lending decision—it had no impact at all.

A last corroboration of the finding that earthquake hazards do not affect property values was a hedonic price analysis performed by Palm (1981b) in three housing markets—Berkeley, Southern Alameda County, and Contra Costa County. In this study, Palm conducted hedonic estimates of the impact of location within a surface fault rupture zone on house price in 1972 (before the disclosure legislation went into effect) and 1977 (a year after it was in effect). Independent variables included square footage of dwelling space, age, quality, and condition of the house, size of the lot, and presence of amenities (swimming pool, fireplace, or view). In addition, data on the economic composition of the area and percentage of single-family dwelling units were included in the equation. Results were not consistent: houses within the Special Studies Zone showed no price effect for their location in Southern Alameda County or Berkeley, but did suffer a $4,182 penalty in Central Contra Costa County. Thus, some evidence indicated that buyers were avoiding surface fault rupture zones in one of the areas, weakening house prices, but this evidence was not overwhelming, and it was not supported in two of the three study areas. Palm concluded that surface fault rupture zonation and its disclosure by real-estate agents had little or no impact on the operation of the housing market.

Summary

Property is an essential part of both the ideology and the economy of California. Owner-occupancy has a symbolic as well as an economic value: owner-occupiers generally hold a higher social status than renters and the federal system of taxation has rewarded owner-occupiers who purchase housing through mortgage financing. In addition, property has usually been an outstanding investment in California, netting returns of 500 percent to some purchasers.

California residents are aware of the environmental risks facing their state. In addition, appraisers and lenders are aware of the potential destruction of property that would accompany a major, damaging earthquake. However, what we see empirically is that despite this awareness by all parties, environmental risk—and particularly seismic risk—has not been integrated into market values. Appraisers and lenders tend to discount or ignore the threat to the property from seismic events, and house prices in areas particularly susceptible to earthquake damage are generally not negatively affected by location.

4

Results of the Pre–Loma Prieta Study

Summary of Findings

In summer 1989, Palm and others (1990) undertook a study to determine the general patterns of adoption of earthquake insurance and other mitigation measures. This study was completed before the Loma Prieta earthquake of October 1989 and also before new legislation was introduced in California to mandate small earthquake insurance policies to cover the deductible. Since this study forms the baseline against which the current research reported here was done, we will review its findings.

Research before the 1989 study suggested that (1) few owner-occupiers purchase earthquake insurance (Kunreuther et al. 1978); (2) those living at greater geophysical risk based on proximity to a major active fault are more likely to purchase insurance—a phenomenon known to insurers as "adverse selection" (Stewart Economics 1989); (3) those more aware of the risk, based on previous experiences with earthquakes or length of residence in California, are more likely to purchase insurance (Kunreuther et al. 1978, Laska 1986, Burby et al. 1988), and (4) those with more to lose—with relatively higher net equity in the property and with more discretionary income to spend on insurance, as well as those with a shorter earning future (the elderly)—are more likely to purchase insurance (Anderson and Weinrobe 1981, Schiff 1977). Those findings formed the basis for the 1989 research design.

Research Hypotheses

The research hypotheses tested in the 1989 study were based on expectations from previous theoretical and empirical work: (1) people living closer to a fault, within a Special Studies Zone, or within a neighborhood susceptible to high-intensity shaking are more likely to purchase earthquake insurance; (2) older persons, those who have more equity in their homes, or those in some combination of these categories are more likely to purchase insurance, and (3) those with higher perceived risk (whether or not they are living in areas of higher actual geophysical risk) are more likely to purchase insurance.

Methodology

A mail survey of approximately 3,400 owner-occupiers of single-family dwellings was conducted in four California counties—Contra Costa, Santa Clara, Los Angeles, and San Bernardino (fig. 1). The survey followed Dillman's Total Design Method (Dillman 1978). A geographic information system (GIS) was used to geocode and analyze the spatial patterns of insurance subscription. Statistical tests and graphical methods were used to examine the research hypotheses.

This study was limited to single-family, detached, owner-occupied homes. Condominium dwellers were excluded from this sample because collective insurance decisions by a homeowners' association involve negotiations and group interactions that confound the simple decision process. Similarly, renters were not included in the sample since tenants do not decide whether to insure a structure against earthquake damage. Finally, the survey was restricted to owners who actually lived at the site. A random sample was drawn from tax assessors' lists of the entire population of owner-occupiers in each study county.

The Survey

A thirteen-page questionnaire was designed, evaluated, and modified using an advisory committee, a field test, and a focus group. An advisory committee composed of university, state and federal government, and insurance industry representatives met twice during the study to develop and evaluate the survey instrument as well as to critique the study methods. The questionnaire was field tested in Contra Costa County using eighty homeowners. A focus group of twelve homeowners assisted in refining the survey questions; each received an honorarium of twenty-five dollars for participation. The survey was modified in response to their invaluable suggestions, opinions, and perceptions.

The Total Design Method (TDM) approach of mail surveys promises astoundingly high response rates (greater than 70 percent). The key portion of the TDM is a sequence of mailings and follow-ups designed to increase response rate. The survey involves four mailings: (1) the initial mailing of the cover letter and questionnaire; (2) seven days later, a postcard thanking respondents and reminding nonrespondents to return questionnaires; (3) twenty-one days after the initial mailing, a letter and replacement question-

Table 3. Response rates to the mail survey

Survey status	Contra Costa	Santa Clara	Los Angeles	San Bernardino
Mailed out	864	855	743	683
Returned to sender	99	61	158	98
Mailed back*	521	556	337	372
Response rate	68.1%	70.0%	57.6%	63.6%

*Does not include surveys refused or returned to sender.

naire to nonrespondents; and (4) forty-nine days after the initial mailing, a letter and replacement questionnaire to nonrespondents by certified mail. Each step increases the response rate. Our study modified the TDM and pretested this modification. Instead of an automatic third mailing after twenty-one days, as specified in the classic Dillman model, the respondent was contacted by telephone. Response rates for the full mail survey varied from a high of 70.0 percent in Santa Clara County to a low of 57.6 percent in Los Angeles County (table 3).

Homeowner Geographic Characteristics

The survey sample was geocoded either by the individual county's GIS center (if available) or by a private contractor. The GIS centers of Santa Clara and Los Angeles counties performed the geocoding for their respective samples, and Geobase, Inc., performed the geocoding for San Bernardino and Contra Costa counties. Updated street address files were used in the address matching process.

This study examined the relationship of insurance purchase and perceived risk with the location of the residence with respect to nearby Special Studies Zones, the San Andreas fault Special Studies Zone, and the maximum potential shaking intensity (such models were available only for Los Angeles and San Bernardino counties) at a given site. The cartographic representations of the Special Studies Zones were digitized from copies of the original 1:24,000 scale topographic maps upon which the zones were compiled. The turning points (critical points) of each zone were digitized, producing a polygonal set of zone boundaries. The euclidean distance from each surveyed homeowner's geographic location to the nearest Special Studies Zone was computed, as well as the distance of each survey residence in Contra Costa and San Bernardino counties to the San Andreas Special Studies Zone. A simple point-in-polygon test was used to determine whether the residence was inside or outside a Special Studies Zone.

Evernden and Thomson's (1985) maximum potential shaking intensity map was recorded by digitizing the Modified Mercalli Intensity class boundaries on the 1:250,000 scale map sheets. The maximum potential shaking intensity at a residence site was derived by assigning the Modified Mercalli Index category to a small area (represented as a polygon) containing that residence.

Results

Analyses of Locational Effects. The relationship between location with respect to these geophysical risks and insurance purchase was explored using t-tests. A significance level of .05 was used to reject the null hypothesis that there was no difference between the average distance of insured and uninsured homeowners to the nearest Special Studies Zone within each county. A similar test was conducted for homeowners in San Bernardino and Santa Clara counties and their distance to the San Andreas fault. Results from the t-tests indicate that no statistically significant relationship exists between insurance purchase and distance to the nearest Special Studies Zones for any of the study counties (table 4). Similarly, no significant relationship was found between insurance purchase and distance to the San Andreas fault for homeowners in Santa Clara and San Bernardino counties.

The relationship between the maximum potential shaking intensity at the home location and insurance purchase was also probed using chi-square tests. Such comparisons suggest that insurance subscription in Los Angeles and San Bernardino counties is not affected by maximum potential shaking intensity.

Finally, isoplethic maps were created to examine the spatial variations in insurance purchase. A surface indicating the percentage of homeowners insured was created for the Los Angeles region, using a spatial interpolation model (the general inverse distance weighted model) to test for other hidden locational effects (fig. 3). The isopleths represent the percentage of respondents who had purchased earthquake insurance. The region of highest percentage insured (60 to 80 percent) is in the San Fernando Valley, whereas only 30 to 40 percent of the homeowners in southeastern Los Angeles County are insured. This spatial pattern may indicate homeowner response to the 1971 San Fernando earthquake.

In summary, the statistical analyses of homeowner location with respect to distance from the Special Studies Zones or the San Andreas fault and

Table 4. Significance of t-tests between distance to Special Studies Zones and insurance purchase

Distance	Contra Costa	Santa Clara	Los Angeles	San Bernardino
To nearest SSZ	.30	.78	.26	.07
To San Andreas fault	*	.32	*	.10

*Not applicable.

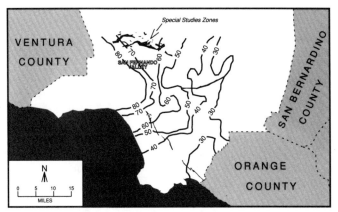

Fig. 3. Percentages of insured homeowners in the study area of Los Angeles County.

with respect to maximum potential shaking intensity all indicated that such locations and the resulting geophysical risk are not associated with patterns of earthquake insurance purchase at the metropolitan scale. However, the spatial modeling of the insurance status surface for Los Angeles County suggests that some relationship may exist between experience and insurance subscription.

Equity, Age, and Insurance Purchase. Previous research suggested a positive relationship between equity and the purchase of insurance, as well as between age of the homeowner and the purchase of insurance (Anderson and Weinrobe 1981, Willinger 1989, Schiff 1977, Arrow 1970, Turner et al. 1980, Hodge et al. 1979, Drabek 1986). Percentage of equity was defined as the market value minus the total claims against the property (e.g., total outstanding mortgages), divided by the market value. The percentage of total net worth of the household represented by this net equity was also examined. Net equity was the major component of total net worth for most respondents, constituting at least 50 percent of net worth in all study counties for both insured and uninsured populations. However, t-tests indicated that percentage of equity in the house and percentage net worth made up by home equity were generally unrelated to insurance purchase (table 5). Only in Contra Costa County was percentage of net equity related to insurance purchase, and even there the percentage of total net worth made up by this net equity was unrelated to insurance purchase. Therefore, the home equity position generally did not differentiate between insured and uninsured households.

On the average, heads of households in the survey were in their late forties to mid-fifties, with the older homeowners in Los Angeles County (fifty-five years for insured and fifty-four for uninsured) and younger home-

Table 5. Significance levels of t-tests for insurance purchase

Variables	Contra Costa	Santa Clara	Los Angeles	San Bernardino
Percentage of net equity	.02*	.74	.26	.57
Net equity as % total net worth	.25	.92	.24	.87
Age of head of household	.00**	.96	.81	.44
Length of residence in CA	.86	.16	.60	.19
Length of residence in home	.15	.50	.75	.99
Age of house structure	.72	.05*	.33	.98
Years of education	.10	.74	.00**	.03*
Children in household	.00**	.38	.08	.96
Persons over 65 in household	.34	.82	.71	.03*
Estimated home value	.95	.05*	.10	.41

*Significant at the .05 level.
**Significant at the .01 level.

owners in San Bernardino County (forty-eight for the insured and forty-nine for the uninsured). Age of head of household did not distinguish between insured and uninsured except in Contra Costa County, where older homeowners were more likely to purchase insurance. In general, however, in the four study counties, the age of head of household cannot be regarded as a predictor of insurance purchase.

Other socioeconomic and demographic variables—including length of tenure in California, length of tenure in the home, age of the house, years of school completed, presence of children under age eighteen in the household, presence of persons over age sixty-five in the household, family income, and estimated home value—were also tested for differences between insured and uninsured frequencies (table 5). Scattered relationships were evident between insurance purchase and these variables. For example, insured households were less likely to include children under age 18 in Contra Costa County, and persons with more years of school completed were more likely to have insurance in Los Angeles and San Bernardino counties. In addition, family income was related to insurance purchase in Santa Clara and San Bernardino counties. However, no consistent relationships were evident across the four counties between these socioeconomic and demographic variables and insurance purchase.

Finally, second-order relationships between insurance and the key independent variables, such as age of head of household, percentage of equity, family income, and percentage of total net worth comprised by the net equity were investigated. Relationships were complex. Only in Contra Costa County did the relationship between age and insurance purchase, which was significant as a first-order relationship, hold up when controlling for income, equity, and net worth. In the other three study counties, no statistically significant relationship was found between age and the tendency to purchase insurance when controlling for the economic characteristics of the household (table 6). Similarly, percentage of home equity did not generally discriminate purchasers from nonpurchasers when controlling for age, income, or net worth (table 7). In sum, the key independent variables were not systematically related to the insurance purchase decision. Even when modified for a second-order relationship, no consistent pattern was seen between demographic or economic characteristics and insurance purchase behavior.

Perceived Risk and Insurance Purchase. Although geophysical risk does not predict insurance purchase, previous research has suggested that perceived risk may be an important factor in the purchase decision (White and Haas 1975, Drabek 1986, Turner et al. 1979). Palm et al. (1990) tested for relationships between risk perception with actual geophysical risk and risk perception with insurance purchase. To measure perceived risk, the survey included four questions. The first asked for an estimate of the probability that a major earthquake (comparable to the 1906 San Francisco earthquake) would occur in the next ten years in the respondent's community. The second requested an estimate of the likelihood that the respondent's own home would be seriously damaged by such an earthquake. The third question elicited an es-

Table 6. Partial correlations for age of head of household and insurance purchase (R-square and significance levels)

Age, controlling for:	Contra Costa		Santa Clara		Los Angeles		San Bernardino	
	R	(sig.)	R	(sig.)	R	(sig.)	R	(sig.)
Income	-.18	(.00**)	-.04	(.21)	-.11	(.07)	-.01	(.47)
Equity	-.11	(.03*)	-.02	(.34)	-.01	(.44)	-.01	(.47)
Net worth	-.17	(.00**)	-.02	(.38)	-.05	(.24)	.03	(.32)

*Significant at the .05 level.
**Significant at the .01 level.

Table 7. Partial correlations for home equity and insurance purchase (R-square and significance levels)

Home equity, controlling for:	Contra Costa		Santa Clara		Los Angeles		San Bernardino	
	R	(sig.)	R	(sig.)	R	(sig.)	R	(sig.)
Age	-.03	(.26)	.01	(.41)	-.08	(.14)	-.11	(.05*)
Income	-.15	(.01**)	-.02	(.37)	-.12	(.05*)	-.09	(.09)
Net worth	-.15	(.01**)	-.00	(.49)	-.11	(.07)	-.07	(.16)

*Significant at the .05 level.
**Significant at the .01 level.

timate of the probability of an earthquake causing more than 10 percent damage to the home. And the fourth asked for an estimate of the dollar value of
probable damage to the home and contents following a major, damaging
earthquake. Kunreuther et al. (1978) posed three of these questions in an earlier survey of hazards insurance purchase.

Respondents indicated a high overall concern about a damaging earthquake affecting their community. In Los Angeles County, for example, 68.9
percent said there was at least a one-in-ten chance of an 8.2 M earthquake affecting their community in the next ten years; in Santa Clara County (the site
of the 1989 Loma Prieta earthquake that occurred shortly after the survey),
23.8 percent estimated that a major earthquake would cause $200,000 or more
in damage to their homes and contents.

These measures of perceived risk were unrelated either to geophysical
risk (proximity to a fault, location in a Special Studies Zone, or location in an
Evernden risk zone) or to economic and demographic characteristics. For
example, the calculated coefficient of determination between distance to the
nearest Special Studies Zone and estimated probability of a damaging earthquake affecting the community ranged from -.01 in Contra Costa County to
-.09 in San Bernardino County. Clearly, individual perception of risk is not affected by proximity to a fault or predicted patterns of earthquake damage; either individuals are unaware of the underlying distribution of risk or they are
not interpreting this pattern in the same way that scientists would.

Despite the lack of relationship between geophysical and perceived risk,
a consistent relationship was found between the belief of personal vulnerability and the adoption of earthquake insurance. In three of the four counties,
the insured population estimated the probability of a damaging earthquake affecting the community and the home as higher than did the uninsured population. In all four of the study counties, the insured estimated the likelihood
of their own home being seriously damaged by an earthquake higher than did
the uninsured (table 8). Finally, in all four counties the insured population
estimated dollar damage from a major earthquake higher (table 9). Thus,
most Californians surveyed were highly aware of the earthquake risk.
Further, a strong and consistent relationship is evident between perceived
risk and insurance purchase.

Conclusions of the 1989 Study. Palm drew four major conclusions from
the 1989 survey. First, insurance purchase rates clearly have increased over
the past seventeen years. The reasons for this increase probably include mandated disclosure of the availability of earthquake insurance; increased awareness of the earthquake risk and the use of insurance as a mitigation measure
resulting from information campaigns; and the inflation of house values and
the need for property owners to protect their increased equity with insurance.
Second, no evidence supports the theory of adverse selection, at least at a

Table 8. Risk perception and insurance purchase: Likelihood of serious damage to home from a major earthquake (summarized as percentage of respondents by insurance status)

	Contra Costa	Santa Clara	Los Angeles	San Bernardino
Very likely				
Insured	3.4	8.3	10.7	24.4
Uninsured	3.6	3.2	13.8	11.0
Somewhat likely				
Insured	40.4	48.5	55.3	51.2
Uninsured	24.2	23.7	37.6	36.2
Somewhat unlikely				
Insured	34.8	31.4	19.1	16.3
Uninsured	29.8	30.8	22.1	22.1
Very unlikely				
Insured	21.3	11.8	11.7	8.1
Uninsured	42.4	42.3	29.5	29.9

Note: The difference between insured and uninsured is significant at .01 for all study counties.

Table 9. Risk perception and insurance purchase: Estimated dollar damage to home from a major earthquake (summarized as percentage of respondents)

	Contra Costa	Santa Clara	Los Angeles	San Bernardino
Less than $10,000				
Insured	4.0	4.5	4.5	6.5
Uninsured	11.8	17.2	20.6	16.6
$10,000-$50,000				
Insured	17.3	20.8	22.2	28.3
Uninsured	26.5	25.6	27.0	34.6
More than $50,000				
Insured	78.7	74.5	73.3	65.4
Uninsured	61.6	57.1	52.5	48.9

Notes: The responses to this question have been categorized for reporting purposes. The difference between insured and uninsured is significant at .01 for all study counties.

metropolitan scale. Those at relatively greater risk have no more propensity to purchase earthquake insurance than those at lesser risk. Thus insurance industry fears of local adverse selection are unfounded by empirical reality. Third, insurance purchase is unrelated to age, income, or ethnicity of the homeowner, to house construction type, or to the distribution of objective risk. Fourth, and most telling, insurance purchase is primarily predicted by the attitude of the homeowner concerning the likelihood of a major damaging earthquake: perceived risk is the most important variable in predicting the purchase of earthquake insurance.

The research reported here has implications for current public policy discussions. First, the finding that insurance purchase is not related to socio-economic characteristics implies that all homeowners regardless of income or age are vulnerable to major uninsured losses. Thus any plan to subsidize or mandate earthquake insurance will affect all segments of the population. Second, the finding that geophysical risk is not associated with insurance purchase suggests that federal, state, and local information campaigns to inform Californians about site-specific risks have not resulted in hazard mitigation behavior. Third, to induce hazard mitigation, it is important to personalize the understanding of vulnerability: if individuals feel more personally vulnerable they are more likely to take mitigation measures, including the purchase of insurance.

Unanswered Questions

The conclusions of the 1989 study leave several questions unanswered. The most important deals with the effects of experience with an earthquake on risk perception and the adoption of mitigation measures against future earthquakes. An analysis of the distribution of earthquake insurance indicated a pattern of higher purchase rates in the San Fernando Valley of Los Angeles County (fig. 3). Since this area was damaged by the 1971 San Fernando (Sylmar) earthquake, damage or experience with an earthquake may have induced greater awareness of the dangers of earthquake damage and therefore led to the adoption of mitigation measures.

For this reason the 1989 Loma Prieta earthquake near Santa Clara County provides an opportunity to test the impacts of experience with a major damaging earthquake on hazard perception and mitigation. This earthquake occurred within the study area of the 1989 sample, enabling the researchers to resurvey each respondent after the earthquake and compare attitudes and behavior before and after. The remainder of this book will be devoted to an explanation of this research, focusing on the relationship between different levels of experience and perception, geophysical knowledge, and mitigation adoption.

5

Insurance Purchase and Risk:
The Development of Research Hypotheses

Before the 1989 survey, a number of relationships had been suggested between individual variables and insurance purchase. Empirical analysis of the 1989 data showed that several of these relationships did not exist among the survey population. For example, the elderly were no more likely to buy insurance than the young, and the very wealthy no more than the less wealthy. The major area that remained to be explored was the possible impact of experience with an earthquake on both attitudes and behavior.

Previous social science research in other contexts suggests that experience does affect both perception and behavior. In this chapter we review the research showing the relationships between insurance purchase patterns and awareness of geophysical risk, experience with the hazard, and perception of vulnerability. We then outline the resulting research hypotheses for our 1990 study.

Expected Purchase Patterns

Awareness of Geophysical Risk

Proximity to a hazard should induce awareness of the risk associated with particular locations. The operating mechanism here is experience or familiarity with the area: persons who live in an area that has suffered a particular form of natural disaster are expected to be more aware of the risk and therefore more likely to adopt mitigation measures such as insurance purchase. This association between distance, awareness, and mitigation has been demonstrated for flood hazards. For instance, in a Denver area study Montz

(1982) suggested that distance of a home from flood zones is an important factor in flood insurance adoption and flood-proofing.

Since many of the 1989 respondents had no previous personal experience with a moderate or major earthquake, we examined the relationship between distance from the active faults and perceptions and behavior, on the assumption that proximity would of itself increase the awareness of potential risk. We hypothesized that homeowners who live near active faults but whose own homes were not damaged are more aware of the geophysical hazards or believe themselves to be at greater risk than homeowners located further from those faults.

Experience with the Loma Prieta earthquake may have affected the homeowner's perception of where the geophysical risks are located, particularly with respect to their homes. This experience may have prompted the homeowner to seek information about earthquake hazards or to pay more attention to information provided by the mass media. In California, three location variables were used to measure the impacts of location on mitigation behavior: proximity to the San Andreas fault, location within or near a Special Studies Zone, and location with respect to the mapped shaking intensity regions.

San Andreas Fault. One of the most widely known active faults in the United States is the San Andreas fault zone (see fig. 1). No other fault in the United States so clearly embodies the idea of earthquake risk. In the San Francisco Bay region, the fault rift is marked by such geophysical features as San Andreas Lake and Bodega Bay. Since this fault system has widespread notoriety, the relative distance between the homeowner and the San Andreas fault might be expected to affect hazard mitigation, particularly following an earthquake along that fault system.

Special Studies Zones. A second type of geophysical risk zone is the Special Studies Zone. These zones were delimited in accordance with the Alquist-Priolo Special Studies Zones Act (California Public Resources Code, Sec. 2623). A Special Studies Zone bounds a fault that is "sufficiently active and well-defined" (Hart 1985). With some exceptions, potentially active faults have shown evidence of surface displacement during quaternary time (the last two million years). Faults that have evidence of Holocene surface displacement (during the last 11,000 years) are deemed "active." A fault is "well-defined" if its trace is clearly detectable by a trained geologist as a physical feature at or just below the ground surface. The Special Studies Zone boundaries are positioned from 200 feet to 660 feet away from fault traces to accommodate imprecise fault locations.

In 1975 the Special Studies Zone Act was amended to mandate the disclosure of the location of a property within a Special Studies Zone to a prospective buyer. The amendment placed the burden for disclosure on the real-estate agent or on the seller, if acting without an agent.

Disclosure became standardized by 1977, and the California Association of Realtors developed a contract addendum to the deposit receipt for California realtors (Palm 1981b). Several boards of realtors printed colored maps outlining the locations of Special Studies Zones, which they used in their offices or gave to clients. Special Studies Zones are also delineated on popular street atlases. Thus, it could be assumed that buyers of property within the surface fault rupture zones were aware of their location. Following an earthquake, these people might be more likely to purchase earthquake insurance.

Microzonation of Shaking Intensities. A third and more rigorous evaluation of the distribution of seismic risk for the study areas in southern California is based on the modeling of possible future earthquakes, their associated magnitudes and rupture lengths, and local ground conditions that may attenuate or amplify the shaking intensity. Evernden and Thomson (1985) mapped the maximum potential shaking intensity for eighty-seven postulated earthquakes in the Los Angeles–San Bernardino metropolitan areas. The postulated Modified Mercalli Intensities (MMI) ranged from less than MMI 5.0 (no damage to structures) to MMI 9.0 (severe damage to most structures). Although the Evernden-Thomson microzonation of risk is probably the most accurate of the three estimates of objective risk, homeowners are less likely to be aware of this zoning and therefore the risk associated with their individual site. Unless detailed maps of shaking intensities are distributed following an earthquake, homeowner behavior or perception change is unlikely to be affected by this distribution of objective risk.

Experience with Hazard

Experience with the hazard is not identical to proximity but may be closely related to it. Thus, experience with the hazard in the current or previous residences should be measured independently for its effect on either perception or adoption of mitigation measures.

In studies of flood hazards, previous experience was found to be the key factor motivating property owners to take steps to mitigate the hazard (Kunreuther et al. 1978, Laska 1986, Burby et al. 1988). Individuals with previous experience of hazards have a more accurate perception of them (Kates 1971, Burton and Kates 1964, Roder 1961, Saarinen 1982), and proximity to hazards tends to cause higher levels of concern (Greene, Perry, and Lindell 1981). Attitude, behavior, and the adoption of mitigation measures seem to be related to experience (Weinstein 1989a).

What mechanism links previous experience with changes in perception and behavior? Research reviewed by Weinstein (1989a) suggests that eight factors may be involved. First, personal experience may affect the perceived likelihood of future victimization, since accessibility from memory influences probability judgments, unless the risk is believed to be cyclical and therefore expected to be lower after victimization (Kahneman and Tversky 1979; Perloff 1983; Slovic, Kunreuther, and White 1974). This factor means that those who suffered damage or inconvenience from the Loma Prieta earthquake should be more likely to believe that they will suffer from future earthquakes, and should therefore have a higher propensity to adopt mitigation measures. However, theory of earthquake prediction poses that earthquakes result from release of accumulated stress along a fault juncture; thus once an area has experienced a major earthquake, it might be expected to be relatively safe for another interval of time. In this case, those who have experienced the earthquake might perceive themselves as safer during the next time period.

Second, personal experience provides information about the possible severity of the harm and the existence of preventative measures. Thus experience with the Loma Prieta earthquake would inform residents of Santa Clara County about the susceptibility of their own homes to even larger potential earthquakes on the San Andreas fault. In addition, the information circulated immediately after the earthquake would increase public awareness of certain mitigation measures and make the insurance decision even more salient.

Third, experience adds to the concreteness of information (Nisbett and Ross 1980). Although homeowners might have understood the possibility of an earthquake in their community, the event itself makes the destruction and inconvenience more obvious. This concrete information should increase attention to the earthquake hazard, possibly also inducing the adoption of mitigation measures. Experience also make events more "available" to recall (Fazio, Zanna, and Cooper 1978), increasing the agreement between attitudes and behaviors (Fazio et al. 1982), so that those already predisposed to adopt mitigation measures are motivated to take action.

Fourth, experience reduces uncertainty about the event (Fazio, Zanna, and Cooper 1978). An imagined earthquake might induce either exaggerated levels of fear or underestimation of the damage and destruction that follows. Experience with an earthquake induces greater certainty about the effects on an individual's family and the susceptibility of one's own property. This increase in certainty about earthquake effects should cause more realistic concern about the risks and the adoption of mitigation measures.

Earthquake experience also increases the salience of an event (Janis 1967, Averill 1987). Again, while a hypothetical earthquake might cause some concern, an actual earthquake in one's own community makes the earthquake hazard real and immediately important. This increase in salience should result in the adoption of mitigation measures.

Sixth, experience with an event, such as an earthquake, is positive demonstration that individuals are not invulnerable (Janoff-Budman 1985, Perloff 1983, Weinstein 1987). This increase in perceived vulnerability, which should occur with damage to one's own property, should induce behavior changes.

Seventh, society exerts an influence on individuals to adopt precautions to avoid further victimization, since individuals may expect blame rather than sympathy if they become victims a second time (Janoff-Budman 1985). This finding follows upon the ideology of privatism: individuals and households are generally regarded as responsible for their own well-being. If an accident or act of God causes destruction, an outpouring of sympathy and aid will follow. However, individuals are expected to take measures to ensure that they are not victims from an identical future accident. This belief in privatism should induce those who have suffered damage to adopt mitigation measures to prevent future victimization.

Finally, previous research shows that specific situations motivate people to attend to messages that may change attitudes (Petty and Cacioppo 1986, Chaiken and Stangor 1987, Doyle et al. 1991). Although federal and state agencies may send out messages about earthquake risk and mitigation measures before an earthquake, they will probably be attended to far more carefully by people who have recently experienced an earthquake. Thus experience with the earthquake may motivate people to attend to public information and change their attitudes to future risk and preventative behavior.

This list of research findings suggests that insurance adoption should be affected by experience with the hazard as well as by proximity to hazardous areas. Those who had direct experience with the Loma Prieta earthquake would be expected to show greater levels of concern with future earthquakes, as well as increased rates of adoption of mitigation measures, including insurance purchase.

Choice Models. Traditional decision theory is based on an assumption that individuals will conduct an analysis of costs and benefits. This theory suggests that individuals make an assessment of the costs of taking or not taking an action, and the associated benefits of their decision. If the calculated benefits exceed the costs, then that rational individual will adopt the action; if the benefits fall short of the costs, then the action is eschewed. Let us consider a very simple example. In the case of earthquake insurance, individuals would tally the risk of an earthquake affecting their homes, and the probable associated dollar losses. If a homeowner estimated that the probability of a major earthquake affecting the home were one in ten, and that the homeowner would lose $300,000 in such an earthquake, then the annualized risk might be calculated at $30,000. If a $300,000 earthquake insurance policy had a deductible of 10 percent (in other words, $30,000) and a premium exceeding

$0, then the individual would not purchase the policy. However, if the calculation was that the probability was 1 in 2, with an estimated annualized loss of $150,000 per year, the deductible was still $30,000, and the annual premium was something less than $120,000, the individual would be likely to purchase insurance. Thus, economists have hypothesized that individual behavior may be understood through an analysis of perceived and real costs vs. benefits of a set of actions.

Finer refinements of this type of calculation predict different outcomes. Examples are suggested by work on "positive responsiveness" and "prospect theory." According to positive responsiveness theory, if the probability of the damaging event (an earthquake) becomes sufficiently small, risk may come to be seen as a mixture of gains and losses. In this case, people will terminate an activity that traditional decision theory indicates should be continued. Thus, demand for risk amelioration (insurance) is reduced (Noll and Krier 1990).

Prospect theory also suggests an outcome different from that of traditional cost-benefit analysis (Kahneman and Tversky 1979). Some relevant aspects of this theory are: (1) that the decision maker derives a value function based on some reference point, (2) that changes in status are more painful as losses than as gains, and that (3) great importance is attached to outcomes that are certain rather than those that are uncertain. Since the event of a moderate-intensity earthquake with little or no damage experienced by the homeowner may create changes in the reference point (the individual estimate of vulnerability), and may suggest new levels of certainty concerning vulnerability to future earthquakes, uninsured status may be seen as having greater utility than insurance purchase. Unstable "decision frames" (Tversky and Kahneman 1981) can also affect the decision to drop catastrophic insurance. Since the decision frame is determined partly by the individual and partly by an external formulation of the problem (e.g., information on probabilities of damaging earthquakes affecting the community), it is possible that small changes in the framing will have significant effects on preferences, sometimes reversing preference structures.

The issue of ambiguity in risk-aversion has been the subject of a great deal of work (Kahneman and Tversky 1979, Ellsberg 1961, Einhorn and Hogarth 1985). Ambiguity obtains when the underlying distribution and frequency of risk is unknown. Many studies have hypothesized an aversion to ambiguity, demonstrating consumer preferences for certain losses or gains and an aversion to uncertainty. A model linking subjective probabilities, ambiguity, and choice has been suggested by Hogarth and Kunreuther (1989). An empirical test of the Einhorn-Hogarth model (1985) suggested that (1) people tend to anchor on an initial estimate of probability and adjust this value by simulating other values the probability could take; (2) increased ambiguity (uncertainty about the true distribution of probabilities) increases the alternative values of the simulated probability; and (3) the relative weights given to alternative values are a function of the individual's attitude toward the ambiguity. Experimental work demonstrated that in the case of low-probability events, consumers showed aversion to ambiguity. In contrast, the experimental work of Camerer and Kunreuther (1989), specifying ambiguity as a second-order probability distribution, showed that their measures of ambiguity had little significant effect on consumer behavior. These findings, along with the work of Schoemaker (1987) on amounts consumers and firms are willing to pay for more precise information on probabilities or losses, are the basis of ongoing research.

Perception of Vulnerability

Perception of vulnerability is theoretically linked with both experience and proximity. However, it should also be considered as an independent factor affecting hazard response. For individuals to respond to a hazard (1) they must be aware of the existence of the hazard and (2) the hazard must be salient to them: they must translate awareness into a belief that their own lives and property are susceptible to danger (Palm 1990).

Previous research shows a relationship between the ways that risks are communicated and their salience to individuals. Three conclusions from this research are particularly relevant. First, the communication must make the hazard memorable. For example, if a risk has extensive media coverage, it probably becomes exaggerated in people's minds. For this reason, individuals overestimate dramatic or sensational causes of death, whereas they underestimate less dramatic, constant, but nonetheless serious ones (Slovic 1986, Lichtenstein et al. 1978). When the media cover an event they create bias that changes public perception of a risk, even when their coverage is accurate. This bias arises because the media tend to dramatize the event (Combs and Slovic 1979). This finding explains why people tend to overestimate the dangers of terrorist attacks or natural disasters and underestimate the impacts of auto accidents or diseases.

Second, since people tend to prefer certainty to probability statements, they reduce the anxiety associated with an uncertainty by denying the existence of low-probability events or by wishfully believing that the hazard is being handled by some external group, such as the government. This desire for zero risk, or "thirst for certitude" (Ruckelshaus 1983), results in a "low tolerance for uncertain formulations of risks and in objections to cautious expressions of scientific knowledge" (Keeney and von Winterfeldt 1986), which in turn make accurate risk communication more difficult.

Third, the presentation of information, or its "framing," can affect its salience, particularly when the audience does not already have strong opinions about the risk (Slovic 1986, Tversky and Kahneman 1981). For example, a real-estate agent can lessen the impact of such information as a house's location near a surface fault by making this disclosure after the client has seen the house, mentally arranged furniture in it, and decided to buy it.

In short, the relationship between communication of a risk and society's attention to that risk is fairly well understood, at least in the short run. This relationship can be manipulated by policymakers attempting to increase or lessen public concern for environmental hazards.

Other studies have investigated the ways in which persuasive communication affects earthquake preparedness. Mulilis and Lippa (1990) showed that California homeowners' scores on an earthquake preparedness scale increased following their reading of negative persuasive communication. However, this negative threat dissipated over a relatively short period of time. The negative persuasive messages in this research were hypothetical—they were not about Californians' own homes, or their neighbors'. In response to the Loma Prieta earthquake, we might expect an intensified reaction to messages about family, neighbors, and friends whose homes were damaged in the earthquake.

Finally, an optimistic bias may distort the relationship between hazard and action. Individuals construct an unduly optimistic bias about safety from a given hazard to create self-serving predictions about future events (Weinstein 1989b). Such a bias "may seriously hinder efforts to promote risk-reducing behaviors" (p. 1232), interfering with the adoption of insurance. The "optimistic bias" might cause individuals to underestimate any future earthquake damage using such arguments as (1) the earthquake struck in 1989 and now we are safe for another hundred years; or (2) our house withstood this earthquake; therefore it is safe against any future earthquake.

In short, previous research has linked experience with the degree of perceived risk. Before an individual responds to a hazard by taking action, the individual must perceive the environmental risk as personally threatening to life and property. Thus, a belief of personal vulnerability is expected to be related to the adoption of a mitigation measure such as insurance. Experience with an earthquake should, in general, increase the sense of personal vulnerability.

Research Hypotheses

The research reviewed above suggests that experience with an earthquake should affect both perception and behavior. This is the primary research hypothesis tested in the current study.

Respondents to the 1989 survey experienced the earthquake in three levels of intensity. First, the Santa Clara County respondents experienced the earthquake directly, through damage to their own homes or to homes in their neighborhoods or community. Second, the residents of Contra Costa County experienced the earthquake through a continual bombardment of newspaper and feature stories as well as through the inconvenience of traffic snarls caused by the temporary closing of the Bay Bridge. Third, the residents of southern California (Los Angeles and San Bernardino County study areas) experienced the earthquake only indirectly. These three levels of intensity of experience in a recently surveyed population of homeowners provided an unusual field design to test for the impacts of experience with an earthquake on the insurance purchase decision as well as on attitude shifts toward personal risk.

Specifically, our 1990 study tested the following hypotheses: (1) the more intense people's experiences are with an earthquake, the greater their belief that an earthquake will impact their homes and communities in the near future; (2) the more intense their experiences with an earthquake, the more likely they are to adopt mitigation measures, including the purchase of insurance; (3) the closer people are to active faults, the greater is their belief that an earthquake will have an impact on their homes and communities in the near future; and (4) the closer people are to active faults, the greater the likelihood that they will purchase insurance and adopt other mitigation measures. In short, the research hypotheses test the effects of intensity of experience with the earthquake and proximity to the active faults on such responses as perception of risk and adoption of mitigation measures.

Summary

The research hypotheses for our 1990 survey are based on the research reviewed in this chapter. Several types of results were anticipated. The resurvey provided longitudinal field testing of theoretical work on the impacts of direct or indirect experience on attitude change and behavior change. The coincidence of a survey followed immediately by an earthquake provided a unique opportunity to extend the resampling methodologies used in other social sciences and in the physical sciences to a study of responses to natural hazards.

The study also involved an additional sampling of owner-occupiers in Santa Clara County to test for the impacts of location with respect to damage as a measure of experience and its effect on perception and response. This test enabled the researchers to calculate the impacts of proximity to damage on both perception and behavior, a variable never before examined.

The opportunity to conduct a longitudinal study with the same individuals provided a window on understanding the process of change in behavior and attitudes associated with varying degrees of experience, holding constant preexisting attitudes, behavior, and demographic characteristics.

Such a study provides new insights into why insurance or other mitigation measures are adopted.

The study is also expected to have intrinsic policy interest. The decision to purchase earthquake insurance continues to be a prominent public policy issue, given the significance of insurance as a mitigation measure and the potential impact of increased insurance purchase on the insurance industry. The study of voluntary adoption of earthquake insurance after a moderate earthquake should inform pending federal legislation that would establish a national reinsurance pool.

6

Study Design

The Loma Prieta Earthquake

The Loma Prieta earthquake occurred on October 17, 1989, at 5:04 P.M. Pacific Daylight Time, dramatically postponing a nationally televised World Series baseball game in San Francisco. The earthquake's epicenter was 16 km northeast of Santa Cruz on the San Andreas fault, and its magnitude was 7.1 (fig. 4). The earthquake was one of the largest to occur in California since 1906. The only earthquakes since 1906 that rivaled the Loma Prieta were the 1952 Arvin-Tehachapi earthquake, the 1940 Imperial fault earthquake, the 1927 earthquake off the coast of Santa Barbara County, and the 1923 Cape Mendocino County earthquake.

The Loma Prieta earthquake resulted in sixty-three deaths and more than $6.0 billion of damage (McNutt and Toppozada 1990). This dollar loss was the largest associated with any natural disaster in the history of the United States.

Damage from the earthquake was widespread: Modified Mercalli intensities of 7 or 8 occurred in San Francisco, Marin, Alameda, San Mateo, Santa Cruz, and Santa Clara counties (fig. 5). Lesser damage was reported in Contra Costa, Solano, San Benito, and Monterey counties. Because the epicenter was in a fairly remote portion of Santa Cruz County, damage was sporadic to built-up areas (McNutt 1990).

Severe damage occurred to the Nimitz Freeway (Interstate 880), the San Francisco–Oakland Bay Bridge and Highway 480 (the Embarcadero Freeway). This damage to freeways and bridges tangled commuter traffic for several

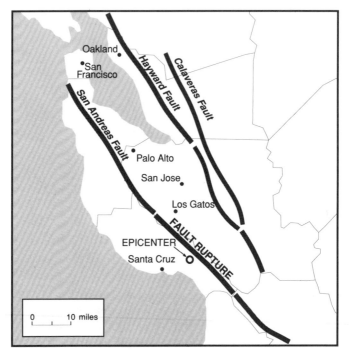

Fig. 4. San Francisco Bay Area, including city locations, fault break, and earthquake epicenter.

months after the earthquake, causing inconvenience to commuters from throughout the bay region. In San Francisco itself, at a distance of 90 km from the epicenter, damage was primarily confined to the Marina District, an area built on bay fill and subject to liquefaction.

Damage was greater in communities closer to the fault break. A higher percentage of structures in communities such as Santa Cruz, Watsonville, and Los Gatos were damaged, with older structures receiving the heavier damage.

Seismologists note that the Loma Prieta earthquake was the strongest experienced by most residents of the Bay Area, but that other segments of California faults have significant probabilities of producing comparable earthquakes during the next twenty years (McNutt and Toppozada 1990). Unfortunately, several of these earthquake-prone fault segments in the Bay Area are located closer to centers of population than was the Loma Prieta earthquake. For this reason, these future probable earthquakes pose an even greater hazard.

Inventory of Losses Associated with the Earthquake

In addition to the sixty-three dead, 3,757 injuries were reported associated with the earthquake, with 368 persons hospitalized. The majority of deaths (forty-two of the sixty-three) resulted from the collapse of the Cypress Structure of Interstate 880. About 12,000 persons were homeless after the earthquake, and several fires—twenty-seven structural fires in San Francisco alone—followed the earthquake. About 23,400 individual homes were damaged and over 1,000 destroyed by the earthquake; 3,547 businesses were damaged and 367 destroyed (BAREPP 1990). The Bay Bridge (which normally handles 250,000 vehicles per day) was closed for a month after the earthquake, and Highway 17 between San Jose and Santa Cruz was closed for thirty-three days by a landslide.

Direct economic losses were estimated at $4 billion in damage to private property and $1.8 billion in damage to public property. Indirect losses, including lost work time, disruption of transportation, and the emotional impact on residents and potential residents, are not calculated in these figures.

Impacts of Loma Prieta on the 1989 Study Area

The earlier survey of homeowners conducted by the authors in the spring and summer of 1989 included two counties in southern California and two in northern California. One of those counties, Santa Clara, was at the

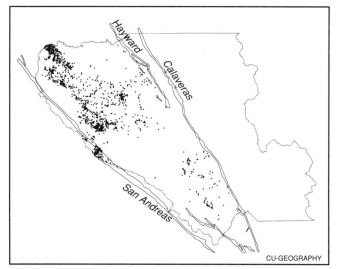

Fig. 5. *Residential damage in Santa Clara County from the Loma Prieta earthquake.*

heart of the area strongly affected by the Loma Prieta earthquake. Another, Contra Costa, was affected less directly: business and residential property suffered less direct damage, but nonetheless traffic patterns were disrupted by the earthquake. Since many Contra Costa County residents commute to San Francisco, the closure of the Bay Bridge caused major disruptions in the daily lives of these households.

Respondents to the 1989 survey experienced the earthquake in three levels of intensity. (1) The Santa Clara County respondents experienced the earthquake directly, through damage to their own homes or to homes in their neighborhoods or community (fig. 5). (2) The residents of Contra Costa County experienced the earthquake through a continual bombardment of newspaper and feature stories as well as through the inconvenience of traffic snarls caused by the temporary closure of the Bay Bridge. (3) The residents of southern California (Los Angeles and San Bernardino County study areas) experienced the earthquake only indirectly, for example, through stories in the news media or communication from friends and relatives living in the San Francisco Bay Area. These different levels of experience in a recently surveyed population of homeowners provided an unusual field design to test for the impacts of direct, less intense, and indirect experience with an earthquake on the insurance purchase decision, as well as on attitude shifts toward personal risk.

Research Questions

Experience with Loma Prieta Earthquake

Research conducted with other natural disasters has shown that experience is a key factor in motivating individuals to respond positively to natural hazards. However, because of the infrequency of large earthquakes, little research has examined the relationship between earthquakes and experience, attitudes, and mitigation activities.

This research documented the county aggregate levels of earthquake insurance adoption, other homeowner mitigation activities, and attitudes toward future earthquakes before and after the Loma Prieta earthquake. As experience is believed to influence the attitudes and response of homeowners to earthquake hazards, changes (or lack of changes) in the attitudes or activities of individual homeowners were examined by comparing their responses on the post–Loma Prieta survey to those on the pre–Loma Prieta survey.

Geographic Location and Damage

While the geophysical risk varied greatly within the major metropolitan areas of California, our previous study demonstrated that adverse selection did not exist. Differential risk does not influence a homeowner's decision to undertake earthquake mitigation activities. The homeowners are either aware of the relative risk associated with their home location and do not respond positively, or are unaware of the relative risk. However, visual analysis of an isoplethic map showed that a greater percentage of homeowners purchased earthquake insurance in the northern San Fernando Valley than in other parts of the Los Angeles study area (fig. 3). This purchase pattern could be related to the location of houses damaged in the 1971 Sylmar earthquake and the subsequent response of homeowners in neighboring areas to purchase earthquake insurance. This possible spatial association suggests that an independent relationship might be present between spatial location and insurance purchase and data on the Loma Prieta earthquake.

This survey explored the homeowner's fundamental awareness of geographic location, the local neighborhood damage, and the relationship of perceived and actual geographic location with attitudes and mitigation activities. Several research questions were posed. Are the homeowners aware of the relative geophysical risk to their homes resulting from geographic location? Does experience (damage to their homes) influence their perceived geographic location? Is perceived geographic risk related to mitigation activities? Do homeowners' direct or indirect experiences with earthquake damage influence their attitudes or mitigation activities?

Study Design

To investigate the research questions posed above, a second mail survey was conducted and the data analyzed using GIS and conventional statistical methods. The new mail survey was used to elicit attitudes and mitigation activities of the previously surveyed homeowners after Loma Prieta. To measure changes in attitudes and mitigation measures, the homeowner responses to the new survey were compared to their previous survey answers. It was expected that only a small percentage (and correspondingly, a small number) of previously surveyed homeowners would have actually experienced damage to their own homes, and that statistical comparisons examining the effects of damage on attitudes and responses would therefore not be valid. To compensate for the expected small damage sample, a new set of homeowners was added to the survey. Santa Clara County offered tax deductions to those homeowners who had sustained at least $5,000 or more structural damage in the Loma Prieta earthquake. Two hundred and fifty of those homeowners were randomly selected and added to the post–Loma Prieta survey population.

One research question explored the relationship between proximity to home damage and attitudes and response. In other words, are homeowners whose homes were not damaged but located near homes sustaining damage more or less likely to believe that their homes are at greater risk to future

earthquakes than homeowners whose neighborhoods were unaffected? To
address this question, an additional set of 500 homeowners was drawn from
the complete population of single-family owner-occupiers using a stratified
random approach. Following a map (fig. 5) of damaged homes (produced
from the county tax relief list), this set of 500 homes was drawn by randomly
choosing homeowners at increasing distances from damaged homes. (Since
actual and perceived distance from damaged homes may not be the same, a
new question addressing the issue of perceived distance was added to the
questionnaire.)

GIS Analysis and Mapping

A geographical information system (GIS) is a system for collecting,
transforming, analyzing, and mapping geographic data. This study and the
previous study used a GIS to determine the geographic location (a process referred to as "geocoding") of each of the surveyed homeowners and damaged
homes in Santa Clara County. Geographic relationships, such as location of a
residential home in a Special Studies Zone or distance from the home to an
active surface fault, were measured with the unique capabilities of a GIS. Finally, a visual analysis of the spatial patterns of insurance purchase, residential home damage, and other factors was conducted by mapping the data.

The geocoding procedure used the TIGER street files available from the
U.S. Bureau of the Census and additional locational files (for the newly developed areas) from the Santa Clara County planning department. The resulting locational accuracy of each home was about fifty feet.

The Total Design Method

The survey methodology followed was the Total Design Method developed by Dillman (1978). The theory behind this method is the "social exchange theory," which suggests that people will be motivated to respond to a
survey because of an understanding that they will receive some kind of return for their actions. Social exchange theory says that people will weigh the
reward that they hope to gain from their actions against the costs of taking
that action, and when they perceive the gain to be greater, they will engage in
the behavior. Therefore, to get the maximum survey response, according to
Dillman, the researcher must (1) maximize the rewards, (2) minimize the
costs, and (3) establish trust. Each of these three steps must be integrated into
the research design.

Maximizing Rewards. One reward is to show personal regard to the respondent. This type of reward is incorporated into the cover letter sent with
the survey, which indicates that the individual was carefully selected and that
the response is needed for the study's success. Other positive ways of showing
personal regard are using real signatures and individualized greetings (e.g.,

Dear Mrs. Jones) on the cover letters, typing letters individually, personally addressing envelopes rather than using address labels, and applying stamps rather than metering postage.

A second mode of reward is to use verbal appreciation, such as "Thank you for participating in this survey." Personal regard is also shown by statements in the cover letter requesting the respondents' opinions; e.g., "It is not known what people like yourself think on these important issues, so we are attempting to find out."

Minimizing Costs. Since time is a major cost, it is important to make the questionnaire as short and as simple to answer as possible. The questionnaire booklet must look inviting and easy to complete. Dillman even specifies a way to fold the materials and insert them into envelopes so that when the respondent opens the envelope, both time and effort are saved.

Personal questions imply a great cost—especially overly direct questions such as those about lifestyle or income. Thus, responses to certain questions (such as "What is your income?") are couched in terms of financial categories ($25,000 to $35,000 per year) so that respondents do not need to answer specifically items they find too personal.

Finally, cost to the respondent is reduced by providing a stamped, self-addressed return envelope so that no money is required to return the completed survey.

Establishing Trust. Dillman's final criterion for success is the establishment of trust. This can be accomplished by including a small monetary payment or offering to send the study results. Another way of establishing trust is to identify the study with a known organization that has legitimacy, such as a state university.

Implementing the Survey. The Total Design Method involves a timetable for contacts with potential respondents. First, the questionnaire and a cover letter are mailed. A postcard reminder is sent a week later. This postcard reminder is directed toward people who want to answer the survey but have set it aside for a few days.

A second mailing takes place twenty-one days after the first mailing. Those people who have not yet responded may be reached by a stronger and more insistent appeal in the cover letter and a reemphasis on the social utility of the survey. At this stage in our survey, if telephone numbers for respondents were available, we made a personal telephone call to emphasize the importance of the survey and ask for a prompt response.

A certified mailing is the last contact with potential respondents. This mailing is sent out forty-nine days after the first contact. The appeal in the cover letter is slightly weaker, but the importance of the response is emphasized because of the increased cost of recontacting the respondent by certified mail. In addition, many respondents must collect the mailing at the post office, further underlining the importance of the survey and their response.

The Advisory Committee

A committee was convened to guide the research team in the design of the survey instrument and to advise on policy issues affecting the research context. This committee included representatives of insurance industry organizations, lobbyists, and insurance regulators, as well as experts in survey research and methodology. The survey questionnaire was modified to incorporate the advisory committee's recommendations.

Resurvey of Households

The first part of the study involved a second survey of those households who responded to the survey on earthquake insurance conducted in spring 1989. The mail survey repeated the questions on the 1989 survey to elicit information on (1) perceived probability of a major damaging earthquake and estimates of associated losses, and (2) demographic characteristics of the household such as number of resident dependents, age of the head of household, length of time the household has had earthquake insurance, and length of time of residence in the region and in the house (see the Appendix). Additional questions probed respondents' experiences with the Loma Prieta earthquake. Since we were seeking information on attitude or behavior change, we used questions identical to those in the 1989 survey. New questions were added about experience with the Loma Prieta earthquake and mitigation responses.

A similar but shorter questionnaire was mailed to the new sample of 750 homeowners in Santa Clara County. This questionnaire focused on experience with the earthquake, locational variables, attitudes to earthquake hazards, and mitigation measures adopted.

Response Rates

The response rates to the resurvey of the respondents in each of the four counties and the supplemental Santa Clara County survey were very high (tables 10 and 11). The lowest response rate was in Los Angeles County, where just over 65 percent of those who answered the questionnaire in 1989 responded to the 1990 questionnaire. The highest response rate was again in Santa Clara County, where 73.7 percent of the respondents to the 1989 survey also responded to the 1990 survey. Seventy-one percent of the homeowners in Santa Clara County responded to the supplemental questionnaire that asked about geographic location and damage. These response rates are approximately the levels predicted for following the Total Design Method.

Table 10. Survey responses to the full mail survey in 1990 and rates compared with the 1989 full mail survey

	Contra Costa	Santa Clara	Los Angeles	San Bernardino
No. of valid responses	308	343	187	233
Total sample*	433	466	287	326
Response rate 1990	71.1%	73.7%	65.2%	71.5%
Response rate 1989	68.1%	70.0%	57.6%	63.6%

*Does not include invalid responses or those returned to sender.

Table 11. Survey responses to the new Santa Clara sample

	Expected damage	Spatially stratified	Total
No. of valid Responses	179	330	509
Total sample*	241	475	716
Response rate	74.3%	69.5%	71.1%

*Does not include invalid responses or those returned to sender.

Test for Response Bias

Since some of the 1989 respondents did not return their questionnaires, we wanted to assure ourselves that we could legitimately compare the 1990 responses with the 1989 responses to seek shifts by county or other subclassification. We therefore compared the two samples on selected variables. When the 1989 respondents were compared with the 1990 respondents using a t-test on the differences in means for age, income, home value, and distance to the nearest Special Studies Zone, we found that the two samples were essentially the same. More technically, the null hypothesis that the means of the two samples were different with respect to age, income, home value, and distance to the nearest Special Studies Zone could not be rejected at the .05 level of significance.

The respondents to the 1989 survey had virtually the same demographic and locational characteristics as the subsample of this group who responded again in 1990. Thus, the 1989 responses can be safely compared with the 1990 responses to seek shifts in attitudes and behavior without concern that the new subsample is in some way unrepresentative of the first sample.

Even with this finding, however, when we are analyzing a shift in attitude, we have selected those 1989 respondents who also answered questions in 1990 for analysis. Only when we are seeking overall changes in behavior (such as percentage of the population who purchased insurance) have we used full population sets for 1989 and 1990.

Summary

Two populations were surveyed in summer 1990. The first comprised the respondents of the 1989 survey in Contra Costa, Santa Clara, Los Angeles, and San Bernardino counties. The second was a new sample of households in Santa Clara County randomly drawn but stratified according to distance from concentrations of damaged housing.

The survey followed Dillman's Total Design Method, with the addition of a telephone call to all households with listed telephone numbers. The response rates were again very high, and the demographic characteristics of the resurveyed population did not differ from those of the original 1989 respondents.

We will now analyze the findings of this survey to answer the major question: What are the impacts of experience with an earthquake on attitudes and behavior? This question will be addressed in the next three chapters.

7

After the Earthquake:
Changes in Attitudes and Behavior

One of the major purposes of the 1990 survey was to test for the effects of experience with the Loma Prieta earthquake on both perceptions and behavior. As indicated in chapter 6, respondents in the four counties differed in their experience with the earthquake. The residents of Santa Clara County were most likely to have experienced direct impacts. Since most damage was focused in this county (and neighboring Santa Cruz County), these respondents were at greatest risk of having their own homes damaged, living in neighborhoods where houses were damaged, or having personal acquaintances who were injured or suffered property damage in the earthquake. This intense experience with the earthquake was expected to yield the greatest shifts in both attitudes toward future earthquakes and measures taken to mitigate against such earthquakes.

The county with the second greatest exposure to the earthquake was Contra Costa County. Here some houses suffered damage, although it was relatively less severe than that in Santa Clara County. Respondents were less likely to have friends or acquaintances who were injured or suffered damage in the earthquake. Contra Costa residents, however, were still closely involved with the earthquake. The collapse of the Cypress Structure on Interstate 880 affected East Bay residents, and the closure of the Bay Bridge for approximately eight weeks snarled commuter traffic to downtown San Francisco and the airport. The local metropolitan newspapers, such as the *San Francisco Chronicle*, carried numerous human interest stories on injuries, damage, and inconvenience caused by the earthquake, as well as predictions of future related damage. Thus, Contra Costa County residents, while usually escaping personal injury or property damage, were closely linked to some direct effects of the earthquake within their metropolitan region.

The residents of the two southern California survey counties were less directly affected by the Loma Prieta earthquake. However, since the San Andreas fault—the same fault on which the Loma Prieta earthquake occurred—passes through their counties, news stories linking their vulnerability to earthquake damage appeared for several months after the Loma Prieta earthquake. The southern California residents were acutely aware of the impacts of this earthquake on their northern neighbors, although they were unlikely to have suffered personal damage or to have been personally acquainted with those who were injured or whose property was damaged.

Following the Loma Prieta earthquake, the attitudes and behavior of homeowners toward earthquake mitigation measures showed both changes and stability. In this chapter, the general behavioral patterns are outlined regarding earthquake insurance purchase, adoption of other mitigation measures, and perceived vulnerability. In chapter 8, more attention will be given to the nature and direction of individual responses.

General Patterns

The post–Loma Prieta survey probed four general topics. First, it examined the variations in experience with the earthquake noted by the sample population, including how directly and intensely the earthquake and its effects were felt. The answers to these questions were used to predict post-earthquake attitude and behavior shifts.

Second, the survey sought to determine the pattern of shifts in the purchase of earthquake insurance. Respondents of interest were those who were insured before the Loma Prieta earthquake but dropped their policies afterward, and those who adopted insurance only after the earthquake. Parameters studied were the number of respondents who changed their insurance status, the locations of their homes, and the justifications they gave for their behavior.

Third, the survey asked about mitigation measures besides insurance that respondents might have adopted after the earthquake. The 1989 pre–Loma Prieta survey showed extremely low rates of investment in such mitigation measures. We wanted to see how such patterns changed after the earthquake.

Fourth, the survey probed shifts in perceived vulnerability to future earthquakes. Here four questions (Appendix, Q-12 through Q-15) asked in the 1989 survey were repeated to ascertain respondents' overall perceptions of vulnerability.

Table 12. Homes damaged by the Loma Prieta earthquake

Level of damage	Contra Costa		Santa Clara	
	#	%	#	%
No damage	266	89.8	141	46.5
$1 - $1,000	23	7.8	110	36.3
> $1,000	7	2.4	52	17.2
Total reporting	296	100.0	303	100.0

Experience with the Loma Prieta Earthquake

Direct Experience

Damage to one's own home, personal injury, or even death are the most intense personal experiences one could have with an earthquake. Although none of our respondents reported deaths in their immediate families, more than 53 percent of the surveyed homeowners in Santa Clara County and 11 percent in Contra Costa County reported monetary losses from damage to their homes (table 12). More than 17 percent of the homeowners in Santa Clara County reported at least $1,000 damage. We expected to see some relationship between this kind of direct experience and changes in attitudes and behavior.

Less Direct Experience

Although the U.S. Geological Survey reported only sixty-three deaths and 3,757 injuries from the Loma Prieta earthquake, 14 percent of the Santa Clara residents and 11 percent of the Contra Costa respondents claimed to have "personally known someone injured" by the earthquake. Not surprising, a much larger number of the surveyed homeowners claimed to have family or friends whose homes were damaged in the earthquake—65 percent in Santa Clara County and 32 percent in Contra Costa County. In addition, more than 60 percent of respondents in these two counties claimed that their travel was inconvenienced as a result of the earthquake.

Residents of the two southern counties in the study did not have direct earthquake-induced experience. However, they experienced the earthquake indirectly through reminders from the news media and local governmental agencies of the potential damage that could result from the active faults in their region.

Experience and Behavior Shifts

Two distinct measures of behavior shift were sought in both the 1989 and the 1990 surveys: insurance purchase and the adoption of other mitigation measures such as structural repairs to the house or the strapping of water heaters. In both surveys, few homeowners invested any money toward earth-quake mitigation other than the purchase of insurance (table 13). In 1990, a larger number of Santa Clara residents reported expenditures for earthquake mitigation measures, but virtually all these respondents were actually report-ing expenses related to damage suffered in the Loma Prieta earthquake. Since the total number of respondents who spent money on other forms of mitiga-tion is so small, we will focus our analysis on the adoption of earthquake insurance.

Between the October 1989 Loma Prieta earthquake and the time of our survey in summer 1990, a total of 65 of the 996 respondents purchased earth-quake insurance. Of these, approximately one-half (32) lived in Santa Clara County. Another one-fourth (16) were in Contra Costa County. In other words, the two northern counties accounted for 74 percent of the respondents who purchased earthquake insurance after the Loma Prieta earthquake.

Before the Loma Prieta earthquake, the insured rate for single-family residential homes in the four study counties ranged from a low of 22 percent in Contra Costa County to a high of 40 percent in Los Angeles and Santa Clara counties (fig. 6). After the Loma Prieta earthquake the insured percentages increased in all four study counties. Santa Clara County, the most directly im-pacted by the Loma Prieta earthquake, registered the largest percentage in-

Table 13. Homeowners' expenditures toward earthquake mitigation (number and percentage of homeowners who made any expenditures)

	Contra Costa		Santa Clara		Los Angeles		San Bernardino	
	#	%	#	%	#	%	#	%
$1-15								
1989	11	45.8	18	48.6	3	25.0	4	40.0
1990	16	50.0	47	58.0	4	40.0	12	63.2
$16-199								
1989	6	25.0	6	16.2	4	33.3	2	20.0
1990	9	28.1	21	25.9	3	30.0	4	21.1
$200 or greater								
1989	7	29.2	13	35.1	5	41.7	4	40.0
1990	7	21.9	13	16.0	3	30.0	3	15.8
No. of households and percentage with expenditures								
1989	24	7.8	37	9.0	12	5.0	10	5.0
1990	32	10.4	81	31.0	10	3.3	19	6.0
Median expenditure								
1989	< $49		$50-99		$100-999		< $50	
1990	< $49		< $49		< $49		< $49	

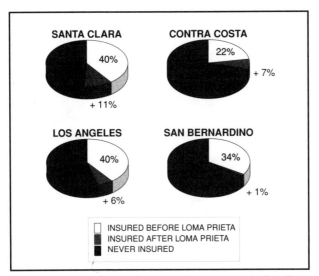

Fig. 6. Insurance status before and after Loma Prieta for all respondents in the four study counties.

crease (11 percent) of insurance adoption, from 40 percent to over 51 percent. In Contra Costa County, the increase was only 7 percent. Los Angeles County showed a 6 percent increase in insurance adoption following the Loma Prieta earthquake, even though its residents were only indirectly impacted by the earthquake. Fewer than 1.5 percent of the survey respondents in any of the four counties dropped insurance after the Loma Prieta earthquake.

Other Mitigation Activities

A homeowner can undertake several other types of mitigation activity to minimize the damage caused by an earthquake. These measures range from bolting bookcases to walls and strapping water heaters to reinforcing chimneys or walls.

After the Loma Prieta earthquake, 31 percent of the Santa Clara respondents and 10.4 percent of the Contra Costa County respondents indicated that they had spent something on such mitigation measures (table 13). In southern California, some respondents had invested in mitigation, although these were fewer than 6 percent in Los Angeles and San Bernardino counties.

Most investment in damage mitigation was small. In all counties about 90 percent of the homeowners taking further action made only minor internal home modifications, such as bolting furniture to walls and floors. More than half of the respondents indicated that these actions cost less than fifteen dollars. As in 1989, the primary reasons for not engaging in more extensive

mitigation activities were that they were "too expensive," that the homeowner "never got around to it," that the measures were "not necessary," or
that they simply "won't help."

Kunreuther and Kleffner (1991) analyzed the justifications that homeowners use for not adopting mitigation measures. Those who consider these
measures too expensive seem to underestimate both the probability of a future earthquake and also the benefits they would obtain from small invest-
ments in such measures. Furthermore, if homeowners focus on the initial
expenditure rather than the long-term benefits—in short, if they use a one-
year rather than a longer-term time horizon for amortizing the expense—
they will not invest in such measures. Although our findings suggest that
there is high concern over a future earthquake and probably little underestimation of its probability or seriousness, we do not have information about
perceived benefits and costs of investing in mitigation measures or the time
frame used in this decision. However, it is likely that this explanation better
accounts for the lack of adoption of voluntary mitigation measures. If voluntary adoption of such measures is sought, it will be necessary to demonstrate
more clearly the long-term benefits and the comparison of these benefits with
the immediate costs. In addition, for those homeowners who indicated that
such actions were unnecessary or wouldn't help, there is need for even more
public information on the kinds of actions that individual homeowners can
adopt and the effectiveness of these actions.

Reasons for Not Purchasing Insurance

Before Loma Prieta

Before the Loma Prieta earthquake, the primary reason in each of the
four study counties for not purchasing insurance was that it was "too expensive" (fig. 7). From 52 to 61 percent of all uninsured respondents in the study
viewed the expense of insurance as the primary reason for not purchasing it.
The second most cited reason for not adopting insurance was that it was "not
necessary"; this answer was given by 19 percent of uninsured homeowners in
Los Angeles County and 34 percent in Santa Clara County. The responses of
homeowners in Los Angeles County differed from those in the other three
counties (fig. 7), in that 11 percent viewed the "high deductible" as the third
major reason for not adopting insurance, whereas only 3 to 4 percent in the
other three counties regarded the deductible as a major concern.

After Loma Prieta

After Loma Prieta, the primary reason for not purchasing insurance
was still that it was too expensive (fig. 8). The percentages for uninsured
respondents in Santa Clara County who said earthquake insurance was too
expensive before and after Loma Prieta were 51.8 percent and 56.5 percent,

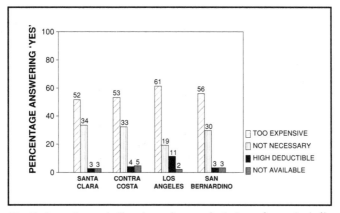

Fig. 7. Percentages of all uninsured respondents in each county indicating reasons for not purchasing earthquake insurance.

respectively. In all counties, a larger percentage of the uninsured after Loma Prieta believed it to be too expensive. Oddly, the greatest increases in this belief occurred in the counties least impacted by the Loma Prieta earthquake—Los Angeles and San Bernardino counties.

In all four study counties, the uninsured group who stated that insurance is "not necessary" (fig. 8) showed a very large percentage decline. Before Loma Prieta 19 to 34 percent of the uninsured county respondents believed that insurance is not necessary, compared with fewer than 7 percent in any county after the earthquake.

Attitudes toward Future Earthquakes

One of the attitude scales used in both the pre– and post–Loma Prieta surveys asked, "How likely do you think it is that your own home will be seriously damaged by an earthquake in the next ten years?" Possible answers were "not very likely," "likely," "unlikely," or "very unlikely." On the basis of simple comparisons between the pre– and post–Loma Prieta responses the four categories were collapsed into two, "likely" and "not likely."

All Respondents

Before the Loma Prieta earthquake in 1989, from 31 to 56 percent of all homeowners believed that a future major earthquake is likely to cause serious damage to their homes (fig. 9). The percentage of homeowners in Santa Clara County (39 percent) and Contra Costa County (31 percent) believing such a damaging earthquake would affect their homes was dramatically less than in the two southern counties, Los Angeles County (56 percent) and San Bernardino County (56 percent).

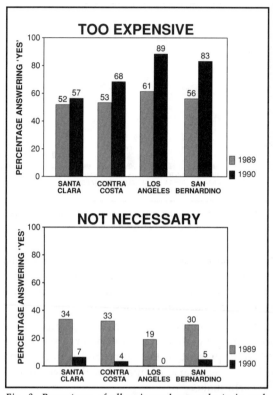

Fig. 8. Percentages of all uninsured respondents in each county indicating that they did not purchase insurance because it was either too expensive or not necessary.

After the earthquake, the fear that a future earthquake would impact one's home increased in all study counties except San Bernardino County. Not surprisingly, the greatest changes in attitudes occurred in Santa Clara County and Contra Costa County.

Insured vs. Uninsured

In the 1989 survey, we found that insured homeowners were more likely than uninsured to expect a major damaging earthquake to affect their homes in the next ten years. After Loma Prieta, these differences between the insured and uninsured widened (fig. 10).

Regardless of insurance status, however, the percentage believing that a future earthquake will damage their homes increased in all but San Bernardino County. The largest percentage increase in concern about future

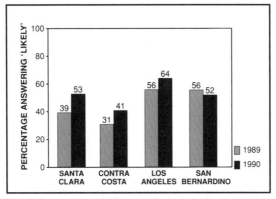

Fig. 9. Percentages of all respondents in each county indicating that a future earthquake is likely to affect their homes.

earthquakes occurred in Santa Clara and Contra Costa counties. However, even after the earthquake, the percentages of homeowners in the two southern counties expecting a future damaging earthquake were still higher than in the northern counties.

Summary

For our random sample of owner-occupiers of single-family detached homes, 53 percent in Santa Clara County and 11 percent in Contra Costa County reported some monetary losses from the Loma Prieta earthquake. More than 17 percent of the homeowners in Santa Clara County reported $1,000 or more of earthquake damage.

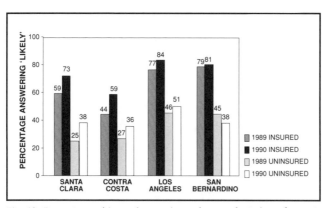

Fig. 10. Percentages of insured vs. uninsured respondents in each county indicating that a future earthquake is likely to affect their homes.

This study also found an increase in the adoption of earthquake insurance. The largest increase for any one county (11 percent) was in that county most impacted by the earthquake, Santa Clara. Here just over 50 percent of all single-family residential homes are now covered by catastrophic earthquake insurance policies. In the other counties, there was little increase in catastrophic insurance subscription, even though fewer than 7 percent of the respondents in any survey county believe that such insurance is not necessary.

8

Changes and Stability in Attitudes and Behavior: The Individual

In chapter 7, we reviewed general patterns of earthquake insurance purchase and the adoption of other mitigation measures, as well as general attitude changes toward vulnerability to future earthquakes. In this chapter, we will focus on shifts in both perceptions and behavior at the individual level. We will consider two primary issues: To what extent did experience with the Loma Prieta earthquake precipitate change in attitudes and behavior, and to what extent were attitudes and behaviors stable despite experience with the earthquake.

We will compare the responses of individuals to identical questions in the pre– and post–Loma Prieta surveys, and assess the direction, magnitude, and correlates of attitude changes. In the first section of this chapter—the investigation of the impacts of experience on change—we will address two questions. First, how does location by county predict behavior change (as indicated by insurance purchase between 1989 and 1990) and shifts in attitudes toward susceptibility to future earthquake damage? We will assume that location (by county) is a surrogate for experience with the earthquake. County location in and of itself is not the focus, but rather the effect that location in Santa Clara County (the site of the earthquake), as opposed to Contra Costa County (where commuting was inconvenienced by the earthquake) or Los Angeles or San Bernardino counties (which experienced no direct impacts of the earthquake), has on behavior. Although we refer to "the effects of county location," we are analyzing the impact of location in a county as a surrogate for a generalized form of experience with the earthquake.

Second, we will address the issue of what characteristics other than county location divide the newly insured from those who remained uninsured. Answers to the first question will indicate for the resurveyed population the impacts of household location in a county on shifts in attitudes and behavior. Answers to the second will indicate the relative significance of location as opposed to other characteristics in triggering changes in insurance purchase behavior.

In the second section of this chapter, we will analyze the characteristics of individuals whose attitudes and behavior remained stable despite experience with the earthquake. Here, we will test for stability in attitude and resistance to behavior change that may have significant implications for the imposition of mandatory mitigation measures.

Behavior and Attitude Change

County Location and Attitude Shifts

On the level of the individual, we investigated attitude shifts, with insurance status held constant. This analysis was used to determine the impacts of experience, as represented by county location, on attitude change within insurance groups. To study this relationship, we disaggregated the county population into three groups based on insurance status: those who have never had earthquake insurance ("never insured"), those who had insurance before the earthquake ("remained insured"), and those who were uninsured before the earthquake but purchased insurance after the earthquake ("newly insured"). We then compared their pre- and post–Loma Prieta estimates of the likelihood of serious damage to their own homes in the next ten years (on a four-point scale from "very likely" to "not very likely"). For Los Angeles and San Bernardino counties, the number of the newly insured population was too small to conduct further statistical analysis.

The null hypothesis is that the estimated likelihood of future damage was the same before and after the Loma Prieta earthquake. A rejection of this null hypothesis would indicate that attitudes had shifted within insurance categories.

In table 14, the null hypothesis is represented by those respondents in the center column—those whose responses showed no change in estimated probability. Those whose estimated probabilities of damage from a future earthquake increased after Loma Prieta are represented in the right-hand column, and those whose probabilities declined are listed in the left-hand column. In Santa Clara and Contra Costa counties, we see the greatest positive shift in estimated likelihood of damage to the respondent's home. Furthermore, the largest positive shifts occurred in the attitudes of the newly insured.

Table 14. Respondents' comparisons before and after Loma Prieta of estimated likelihood of damage to homes in a future earthquake: Net shift from 1989 to 1990

Insurance status	Less likely	No change	More likely
Santa Clara			
Newly insured	6.7	30.0	63.3
Never insured	15.9	55.2	29.0
Remained insured	12.9	54.0	33.1
Contra Costa			
Newly insured	0.0	25.0	75.0
Never insured	14.9	57.4	27.7
Remained insured	15.2	51.5	33.3
Los Angeles			
Never insured	17.4	55.8	26.7
Remained insured	11.9	67.8	20.3
San Bernardino			
Never insured	27.9	46.5	25.6
Remained insured	20.0	60.0	20.0

Although the county contrasts in category shifts (for example, changes in responses from "not very likely" to "somewhat unlikely") by insurance status are not statistically significant, county location did have a significant impact on the overall pattern of change in response (table 15). Thus, for each insurance status grouping, response shifts were similar across the four counties. However, for all respondents taken together, attitude shifts were also independently related to county location.

Summary statistics were also calculated to test for county contrasts in attitude shifts. Analysis of variance was conducted to determine whether county location had an independent statistical effect on the three attitude questions measured on a ratio level, either for the overall sample or when

Table 15. Attitude shifts based on county location within categories of insurance status (Does county location predict attitude shift within insurance categories?)

Difference* between 1990 and 1989 responses to "How likely do you think it is that your own home will be seriously damaged by an earthquake in the next ten years?"

	Chi-square	Probability
All respondents	18.33	.01*
Newly insured	11.02	.09
Never insured	10.18	.12
Remained insured	7.98	.24

*Kruskal-Wallis test (chi-square).

Table 16. One-way ANOVA test to predict attitude shift based on county location within categories of insurance status (Does attitude shift within insurance categories vary by county?)

	F-ratio	F-probability
Chances of a 1906 San Francisco-type earthquake in community in the next ten years (log of 1990-1989 response):		
Total	2.11	.10
Newly insured	.39	.76
Never insured	.88	.45
Remained insured	.61	.60
Chances of a major earthquake causing more than 10 percent damage to own home in next ten years (log of 1990-1989 response):		
Total	1.19	.31
Newly insured	.49	.69
Never insured	1.84	.14
Remained insured	1.18	.32
Dollar damage to the contents of house and structure by a major damaging earthquake (log of 1990-1989 response):		
Total	1.06	.37
Newly insured	.04	.99
Never insured	.76	.52
Remained insured	2.61	.20

subdivided by insurance status (table 16). This test showed that county location did not have an independent effect on such shifts.

In contrast, insurance status was more related, but inconsistently, to attitude shifts within counties. For these calculations, responses before Loma Prieta were compared to responses after Loma Prieta for the same individuals. These response changes were stratified by insurance status (newly insured, never insured, and remained insured) and calculated for the full sample as well as for individual counties. The research question analyzed whether there were significant differences in the stability of attitudes toward earthquakes among persons of different insurance status.

The results (table 17) were statistically significant for the full sample (insurance status predicted attitude shift for all the counties together), but in no case were statistically significant within counties. Thus neither insurance status nor county location is a good individual predictor of attitude shift.

Attitude Shifts: Experience vs. Demographic Characteristics

We conducted another set of tests in order to probe the nature and correlates of attitude shifts. These tests used discriminant models—linear

Table 17. One-way ANOVA test to predict attitude shift based on county location within categories of insurance status (Does attitude shift within counties vary by insurance status?)

	F-ratio	F-probability
Chances of a 1906 San Francisco-type earthquake in community in the next ten years (log of 1990-1989 response):		
Total	6.02	.00
Contra Costa	2.45	.09
Santa Clara	2.73	.07
Los Angeles	.99	.38
San Bernardino	.70	.50
Chances of a major earthquake causing more than 10 percent damage to own home in next ten years (log of 1990-1989 response):		
Total	5.30	.01
Contra Costa	2.67	.07
Santa Clara	.94	.39
Los Angeles	1.92	.15
San Bernardino	2.04	.13

combinations of discriminating variables that maximized the separation of the groups.

Two sets of discriminant functions with fixed variables were calculated. The first was composed of indicators of demographic and socioeconomic status: place of birth (within California or elsewhere), percentage of equity in the home, home value, length of residence in the home, years of school completed, and age of the household head. We labeled this function a "demographic function" in order to capture the idea that variables represented economic, social, and demographic characteristics as opposed to attitudes or experience with the earthquake. Another set included variables indicating experience with the earthquake: damage from the Loma Prieta earthquake, acquaintance with anyone injured in the earthquake, family or friends whose houses were damaged in the earthquake, and distance to the nearest house seriously damaged in the earthquake. This function, representing the experience of the respondent with the earthquake or extent of linkage with others who had experienced the earthquake, was labeled the "experience function."

As might be expected, the experience function performed poorly in all but Santa Clara County. But more surprising, in all four counties the demographic function was consistently better at distinguishing those whose attitudes had shifted—those who believed an earthquake was more likely as opposed to those who believed it was less likely (table 18).

The analysis leaves us with a paradox. Although demographic variables individually or in combination do not distinguish the insured from the

Table 18. Discriminant analysis: Change in response to "How likely is it that your own home will be seriously damaged by an earthquake in the next ten years?"

County	Demographic function	Experience function
Summary statistic: percentage of cases correctly classified by the discriminant function.		
Contra Costa	59.22	50.00
Santa Clara	65.57	63.97
Los Angeles	60.38	42.86
San Bernardino	62.20	53.13

Demographic function: State of birth, percentage of equity in the home, estimated value of the home, length of residence in the home, years of school completed, age of the head of household.

Experience function: Was the house damaged in the Loma Prieta earthquake (yes or no); did they know people who were injured; were houses of family or friends damaged; distance from nearest seriously damaged house.

uninsured or the post–Loma Prieta purchasers (new purchasers) from the never insured, they do distinguish the attitude shifters—those who are more concerned with future earthquakes as opposed to those who are now less concerned. As seen from the discriminant analysis, those respondents born outside California and with more formal education tended to increase their estimated likelihood of a major earthquake damaging their own homes after the Loma Prieta earthquake. Further, these variables in combination with other demographic variables better distinguished attitude changers than did experience variables in each of the four study counties. This finding adds weight to the suggestion that experience with an earthquake has a differential effect within a population.

Experience with the earthquake should affect the population differentially as measured by other outcomes such as insurance purchase or adoption of other mitigation measures.

Differences between the Newly Insured and the Uninsured

As described above, most of the new insurance purchasers after the Loma Prieta earthquake were residents of Santa Clara County. Further, these newly insured households were more likely to have increased their concern about an earthquake affecting their own homes in the next ten years than either those who remained insured or those who did not purchase insurance. What other characteristics distinguish the post–Loma Prieta insurance purchasers from those who remained uninsured even after the earthquake?

We hypothesized that three factors would distinguish the postearthquake insurance purchasers from the nonpurchasers: (1) experience with the earthquake as measured by county location; (2) experience with the earthquake as measured by the extent of damage to one's own home; and (3) perceived risk of future damage from earthquakes. The analysis of the pre–Loma Prieta survey (Palm et al. 1990) showed no consistent relationship between insurance purchase and economic or demographic variables. Therefore, we expected that economic and demographic factors would not distinguish newly insured homeowners from the uninsured.

   Our first analyses were tests to determine the differences between those who did not purchase insurance and those who purchased insurance after the Loma Prieta earthquake, in order to assess the impacts of individual socioeconomic variables on the purchase decision. Differences between purchasers and nonpurchasers were calculated with respect to state of birth (California or other), presence of children under the age of eighteen in the household, value of the home, percentage of equity in the home, age of the head of household, percentage of total net worth (accounted for by home equity), length of residence in California, years of school completed, presence of persons aged sixty-five and older in the household, and family income (table 19). The only variable significantly related to the purchase/nonpurchase classification was home value, and only in Contra Costa and Santa Clara counties. We may therefore conclude that, as in 1989, socioeconomic and demographic variables in general did not distinguish insurance purchasers from nonpurchasers.

   To explore further the relationship of home value, t-tests were calculated for the log of home value—to see if the insured differed from the uninsured with respect to home value, or if only the new insurance purchasers had higher home values than the uninsured. In the two northern counties (Contra Costa and Santa Clara), the insured were not statistically different from the uninsured with respect to home value, but the new purchasers had higher home values than the uninsured (table 20). This analysis suggests that

Table 19. Significance level of tests on differences between newly insured and uninsured

County	State of birth[a]	Children under 18[a]	Home value[b]	Percentage of Equity[b]	Age of head of household[b]
Contra Costa	.189	.932	.002	.447	.574
Santa Clara	.980	.888	.021	.521	.816

County	Net worth in equity[b]	Length of residence[b]	Years of school[b]	Persons over age 65[b]	Family income[b]
Contra Costa	.873	.845	.167	.051	.420
Santa Clara	.459	.433	.434	.085	.908

[a]Chi-square tests.
[b]t-tests.

Table 20. Insured vs. uninsured and new purchasers vs. uninsured: "t-tests" on home value

| County | Significance level for t-tests | |
	Insured/uninsured	New purchasers/uninsured
Contra Costa	.822	.002
Santa Clara	.100	.028
Los Angeles	.296	.499
San Bernardino	.434	.517

the new purchasers seem to be a different population than the full population of insured homeowners.

A second set of analyses was carried out to consider the role of individual variables simultaneously. To identify the set of variables that best discriminates between postearthquake insurance purchasers and nonpurchasers, two sets of statistical tests were performed: logit and discriminant analysis.

In statistical analyses, such as those in our study, logit analysis can be used to estimate probabilities with a dichotomized dependent variable, such as status as insurance purchasers or nonpurchasers (Blalock 1979). This mode of analysis is used where the dependent variable is not continuous, an assumption required by the ordinary least squares (multiple regression) model. As the dependent variable approaches one value or the other, the coefficient of changes in the independent variable (∂X) approaches zero. A set of continuous or dichotomous variables can therefore be used to calculate a function that best distinguishes one value of the dependent variable from the other. In our study, a set of predictor variables (age of the homeowner, perception of risk) is combined to create a statistical function that distinguishes buyers from nonbuyers. The coefficients estimated in the model reflect how values of certain independent variables increase or decrease the probability of the purchase of earthquake insurance. For example, a positive and significant coefficient on the home value variable implies that as home value increases, the probability of purchasing insurance would also increase. A negative and significant coefficient would decrease the probability of purchase as home value increased.

In logit analysis, test statistics are used to determine the significance of individual parameters as well as the power of the full model. A chi-square statistic measures the significance of individual parameters. A 2 x 2 matrix of predicted vs. actual results of the model measures the quality of the model as a whole. This matrix shows the classification accuracy, given the parameters estimated.

The best model for the respondents in all four counties taken together was one using estimated likelihood of home being damaged in both the pre–

and post–Loma Prieta surveys, estimated selling price of the home, estimated damage to the home from a hypothetical future earthquake, and extent of actual damage to home in the Loma Prieta earthquake. This model correctly predicted the answers of more than 80 percent of all respondents and about one half of the insurance purchasers (table 21).

A model for the two northern California counties was slightly less accurate overall in correctly classifying respondents, but was more accurate in predicting those who would purchase insurance (62.5 percent of the latter correctly classified) than in predicting which of those who were uninsured in 1989 would remain uninsured in 1990. This model consisted of the 1989 and 1990 estimates of the likelihood of damage to the home, the assessment on a one-to-five scale of the seriousness of the damage to the house and contents, and an estimate of the home value (table 22).

Discriminant Models

Discriminant analysis was also used to differentiate the newly insured from the uninsured homeowners. For our study, the linear combination of predictor variables (age of homeowner, perception of risk) were combined to distinguish best the newly insured from the uninsured.

The discriminant functions performed somewhat better than the logit models both in overall predictions and in predicting membership in the purchaser group. In order to test the classic benefit/cost explanation for the purchase of insurance, discriminant functions were calculated using variables related to this theoretical model: actual loss from the Loma Prieta earthquake

Table 21. Logit models: Post–Loma Prieta insurance purchasers vs. uninsured: Model for the four-county sample

Variable	Parameter estimate	Standard error	Wald chi-square	Probability of chi-square
Intercept	-15.85	4.39	13.01	.00
Likelihood of home being damaged (1990)	-1.14	0.26	19.65	.00
Likelihood of home being damaged (1989)	0.75	0.23	11.13	.00
Home value (lg)	0.95	0.34	7.97	.00
Perceived level of damage (lg - dollars)	0.22	0.14	2.68	0.10
Loma Prieta damage	0.55	0.39	1.99	0.16
Percentage correctly classified by the model				
Overall	81.3			
Insurance purchasers	50.0			
Nonpurchasers	85.8			

Table 22. Logit models: Post–Loma Prieta insurance purchasers vs. uninsured: Model for the northern county sample

Variable	Parameter estimate	Standard error	Wald chi-square	Probability of chi-square
Intercept	-2.86	1.04	7.66	0.00
Likelihood of home being damaged (1990)	-1.60	0.34	22.63	0.00
Likelihood of home being damaged (1989)	1.27	0.31	17.18	0.00
Home value (lg)	2.83	1.19	5.66	0.02
Perceived seriousness of Loma Prieta damage	0.57	0.32	3.27	0.07
Percentage correctly classified by the model				
Overall	80.7			
Insurance purchasers	62.5			
Nonpurchasers	83.8			

as a percentage of home value, estimated dollar loss from a hypothetical earthquake (perceived vulnerability), actual insurance cost (as reported by the insured and as calculated for the uninsured based on value of the structure), estimated probability of a major damaging earthquake affecting the home, and past experience (damage to the home by a previous earthquake). This function correctly classified 58 percent of the respondents in Contra Costa County and 61.5 percent of the respondents in Santa Clara County (table 23).

Table 23. Discriminant functions: Postearthquake insurance purchasers vs. nonpurchasers: Cost-benefit model (Santa Clara only)

Variable	Ind. Wilks	Standard canonical	Overall Wilks
Percentage of home value perceived to be at risk from future earthquake	.99**	-.04	
Perception of dollar damage to home in hypothetical earthquake	.05	.81	
Cost of insurance	.74	-.04	
Estimated probability of future earthquake	.99**	-.20	
Percentage of home value damaged in LP Earthquake	.14	.60	
Overall Wilks			.95*
Percentage Correctly Classified			
Overall	61.5		
Insurance Purchasers	45.8		
Nonpurchasers	65.1		

*Significant at .05. **Significant at .01.

However, this cost-benefit model did not perform as well as simpler models based on experience: the best model overall for all counties consisted of one variable: the percentage of the home value damaged in the Loma Prieta earthquake (table 24). This model correctly predicted insurance purchase or nonpurchase in almost 82 percent of the cases, with 61.5 percent of the nonpurchasers correctly predicted.

The discriminant function best classifying those who purchased insurance after the Loma Prieta earthquake was composed of the home value and an estimate of the damage the home would suffer in a hypothetical future earthquake. This function correctly classified 71.7 percent of the cases. The function that best approached the full set of theoretical expectations—

Table 24. Discriminant functions: Postearthquake insurance purchasers vs. nonpurchasers: Four-county sample

Variable		Ind. Wilks	Standard canonical	Overall Wilks
BEST OVERALL FUNCTION				
Percentage of home value damaged in Loma Prieta earthquake		.97*	.23	
Overall model				.97*
Percentage correctly classified				
Overall	81.7			
Insurance purchasers	86.6			
Nonpurchasers	61.5			
BEST MODEL FOR PREDICTING INSURANCE PURCHASERS				
Home value (Lg)		.96*	1.04	
Perception of dollar damage to home in hypothetical earthquake		.98*	.99	
Overall model				.94*
Percentage correctly classified				
Overall	65.8			
Insurance purchasers	71.7			
Nonpurchasers	64.4			
BEST MODEL FOLLOWING THEORETICAL EXPECTATIONS				
Percentage of home value damaged in Loma Prieta earthquake		.97*	.76	
Perception of dollar damage to home in hypothetical earthquake		.97*	-.62	
Overall model				.96*
Percentage correctly classified				
Overall	71.5			
Insurance purchasers	51.6			
Nonpurchasers	74.2			

*Significant at .05.

consisting of the extent of dollar damage controlled by home value plus an estimate of the damage the home would suffer in a hypothetical future earthquake—was better at predicting uninsured response (74.2 percent correctly classified). However, this function did not predict membership in the insurance purchaser group as effectively as did the first two models (51.6 percent correctly classified).

Summary of Findings

We hypothesized that variables representing county location, damage in the Loma Prieta earthquake, and perceived risk would best discriminate between newly insured and uninsured homeowners. We found that two of these variables—damage and perceived risk—performed well. County location was not statistically significant in these models, indicating that other surrogates for experience, such as damage measures, were better discriminators. In addition, we found that home value was a good predictor of insurance purchase in the discriminant or logit model, and when considered separately. Further, a set of demographic variables better discriminated among those perceiving greater and less future risk of an earthquake affecting their homes—a factor that has had a strong and consistent correlation with insurance purchase. This finding contributes to the conclusion that the new insurance purchasers were a different population from the original purchasers.

Behavior and Attitude Stability: 1989 to 1990

In the first section, we reviewed the shifts in both behavior and attitudes that occurred after the Loma Prieta earthquake. We found that 64 of 996 of the respondents had purchased earthquake insurance. Further, this population tended to be located in Santa Clara county—the site of the earthquake—and showed a major change in their attitudes toward the likelihood of their own homes being seriously damaged by an earthquake in the next ten years. But what about the 94.6 percent of the survey population whose insurance status was unchanged? And the population whose attitudes toward risk remained stable? In this section, we will examine the extent to which our respondents did not react to the Loma Prieta earthquake and exhibited stability in both attitudes and behavior over this period.

Since such a small percentage (6 percent overall) of insurance adoption followed the earthquake, it is not surprising that there was very little overall shift in either attitude or behavior for most of the variables on which the respondents were measured. Respondents tended to give the same answers to questions in both 1989 and 1990.

Attitudes were measured in two ways. First, we made a direct estimate of the probability of a major damaging earthquake affecting the community and the home and the estimated dollar damage to the home from such a major earthquake. When the mean responses for 1989 were compared with those for 1990 for respondents who remained insured or those who remained uninsured (those 94 percent who did not change insurance status), they tended to show little change (table 25). Despite several counterintuitive findings—that respondents who remained insured tended to indicate a lower probability of a damaging earthquake affecting their community in Contra Costa County, that respondents from Santa Clara County who did not buy insurance predicted a higher dollar damage from such an earthquake, and that respondents in Los Angeles County who did not have insurance indicated a higher probability of a major earthquake affecting their community—by and large, no systematic overall attitude shift occurred for the survey respondents between 1989 and 1990.

Second, we measured attitude shift by response to a set of variables intended to elicit the respondents' reasons for their insurance purchase decision. For example, those who were uninsured in both 1989 and 1990 were asked about the importance of various factors in their decision not to purchase insurance, such as the low probability that an earthquake might destroy their houses, or their having only a small amount of family wealth tied up in the home equity. Similarly, those who were insured in both years were asked the converse: how much such factors as the high probability that an earthquake might destroy their houses, or their having a large investment in home equity affected their decision to purchase insurance.

The first question addressed the degree to which worry about an impending earthquake motivates insurance purchase (table 26). The greatest shift took place in Los Angeles County, where the response to this variable increased both as a reason why the "never insured" refused to buy insurance and as a reason why the "remained insured" continued to purchase earthquake insurance. In the other counties, little or no shift occurred in the importance of this variable in the insurance purchase decision.

A second variable was the extent to which the household values insurance as a protection for most of its wealth, which is primarily in home equity (table 27). Here the responses of neither the purchasers nor the nonpurchasers showed a significant shift in the importance of this variable.

A third factor is the extent to which the cost of insurance is acceptable to the homeowner. The only significant shift in response was for the uninsured in Contra Costa county, for whom cost became an even more important factor in their decision not to purchase insurance in 1990 (table 28).

One of the largest shifts concerned the impact of newspaper maps on those who remained uninsured (table 29). Respondents in all counties indicated that they had a greater tendency to see newspaper maps, which further convinced them that insurance was not justified.

Table 25. Summary of attitude shifts between 1989 and 1990: Reported means and paired-samples t-tests

		Remained insured	Never insured
ESTIMATED PROBABILITY OF A DAMAGING EARTHQUAKE AFFECTING COMMUNITY			
Contra Costa:	1989 Mean	42.74	71.70
	1990 Mean	125.33	95.70
	(ln)t-value	2.63	2.12
	2-tail probability	.01	.04
Santa Clara:	1989 Mean	65.65	91.73
	1990 Mean	42.71	87.66
	(ln)t-value	-.57	1.03
	2-tail probability	.57	.31
Los Angeles:	1989 Mean	24.78	134.49
	1990 Mean	25.78	121.28
	(ln)t-value	-.05	-1.63
	2-tail probability	.96	.01
San Bernardino:	1989 Mean	71.71	103.60
	1990 Mean	34.16	105.84
	(ln)t-value	.21	-.09
	2-tail probability	.84	.93
ESTIMATED PROBABILITY OF A DAMAGING EARTHQUAKE AFFECTING HOME			
Contra Costa:	1989 Mean	113.90	105.50
	1990 Mean	37.34	128.30
	(ln)t-value	2.90	1.01
	2-tail probability	.01	.31
Santa Clara:	1989 Mean	61.94	140.34
	1990 Mean	35.52	132.64
	(ln)t-value	.49	1.31
	2-tail probability	.62	.19
Los Angeles:	1989 Mean	27.05	50.09
	1990 Mean	26.42	163.09
	(ln)t-value	1.09	-.53
	2-tail probability	.28	.60
San Bernardino:	1989 Mean	34.51	93.93
	1990 Mean	22.06	87.06
	(ln)t-value	.44	-1.30
	2-tail probability	.66	.20
ESTIMATED DOLLAR DAMAGE FROM A MAJOR EARTHQUAKE			
Contra Costa:	1989 Mean	145,602	115,830
	1990 Mean	151,768	122,472
	(ln)t-value	.12	-.43
	2-tail probability	.90	.66 *(Continued)*

(Table 25, continued)

		Remained insured	Never insured
Santa Clara:	1989 Mean	163,800	99,051
	1990 Mean	157,250	134,819
	(ln)t-value	-.74	2.32
	2-tail probability	.46	.02
Los Angeles:	1989 Mean	117,388	92,218
	1990 Mean	141,173	103,136
	(ln)t-value	-2.34	-.83
	2-tail probability	.02	.41
San Bernardino:	1989 Mean	110,824	73,272
	1990 Mean	125,088	80,480
	(ln)t-value	-1.41	.45
	2-tail probability	.16	.66

Table 26. Fear of future earthquake as decision motivator

		Remained insured	Never insured
I (DO NOT) WORRY THAT AN EARTHQUAKE MAY DESTROY MY HOUSE OR CAUSE MAJOR DAMAGE IN THE NEAR FUTURE.			
Contra Costa:	1989 Mean	4.00	3.10
	1990 Mean	4.00	3.10
	z-value	-.67	-.08
	2-tail probability	.50	.94
Santa Clara:	1989 Mean	4.30	3.10
	1990 Mean	4.20	3.20
	z-value	-.72	.85
	2-tail probability	.48	.40
Los Angeles:	1989 Mean	4.50	2.80
	1990 Mean	4.10	3.10
	z-value	-2.61	-2.78
	2-tail probability	.01	.00
San Bernardino:	1989 Mean	4.30	3.00
	1990 Mean	3.90	3.20
	z-value	-2.28	-1.29
	2-tail probability	.02	.20

Although newspaper maps increased in importance, the general impact of mass media, such as television broadcasts and news articles, on the insurance purchase decision also showed little change. The statement was posed as: "I watched a television program or read an article on earthquake hazards that convinced me that I needed (did not need) to buy earthquake insurance."

Table 27. Equity in home as decision motivator

		Remained insured	Never insured
MOST OF OUR FAMILY WEALTH IS (IS NOT) TIED UP IN THE EQUITY OF OUR HOUSE, WHICH MIGHT BE LOST IF AN EARTHQUAKE DESTROYED OR DAMAGED IT.			
Contra Costa:	1989 Mean	4.00	2.70
	1990 Mean	3.90	2.90
	z-value	-.50	-1.78
	2-tail probability	.61	.08
Santa Clara:	1989 Mean	4.00	3.10
	1990 Mean	4.00	3.10
	z-value	-.76	-1.04
	2-tail probability	.45	.30
Los Angeles:	1989 Mean	3.90	3.00
	1990 Mean	4.00	3.30
	z-value	-1.15	-1.66
	2-tail probability	.25	.10
San Bernardino:	1989 Mean	4.00	2.90
	1990 Mean	4.10	3.10
	z-value	-.60	-.92
	2-tail probability	.55	.36

Table 28. Cost of insurance as decision motivator

		Remained insured	Never insured
THE COST OF INSURANCE IS ACCEPTABLE/UNACCEPTABLE.			
Contra Costa:	1989 Mean	3.60	4.00
	1990 Mean	3.60	4.30
	z-value	-.10	-2.68
	2-tail probability	.92	.01
Santa Clara:	1989 Mean	4.00	3.10
	1990 Mean	4.00	3.10
	z-value	-1.66	-1.64
	2-tail probability	.10	.10
Los Angeles:	1989 Mean	3.80	4.20
	1990 Mean	3.80	4.40
	-value	-.14	-1.61
	2-tail probability	.89	.11
San Bernardino:	1989 Mean	3.70	4.10
	1990 Mean	3.90	4.20
	z-value	-1.08	-1.25
	2-tail probability	.28	.21

Table 29. Impacts of newspaper maps on decisions

		Remained insured	Never insured
I SAW NEWSPAPER MAPS SHOWING HAZARDS AREAS AND DECIDED THAT I NEEDED (DID NOT NEED) EARTHQUAKE INSURANCE.			
Contra Costa:	1989 Mean	2.30	2.20
	1990 Mean	2.30	2.70
	z-value	-.03	-3.66
	2-tail probability	.98	.00
Santa Clara:	1989 Mean	2.30	2.00
	1990 Mean	2.60	2.40
	z-value	-1.22	-3.25
	2-tail probability	.22	.00
Los Angeles:	1989 Mean	2.00	1.70
	1990 Mean	2.40	2.50
	z-value	-1.21	-3.63
	2-tail probability	.23	.00
San Bernardino:	1989 Mean	2.50	1.90
	1990 Mean	3.10	2.40
	z-value	-2.29	-3.93
	2-tail probability	.02	.00

Responses indicated that in most cases, such information was relatively unimportant (scores less than 3), and only in San Bernardino County did the impact of this factor on both purchasers and nonpurchasers increase significantly. This finding may account for the small increase in insurance adoption in San Bernardino County compared to a larger increase in neighboring Los Angeles County.

A factor that increased in importance to the insurance purchase decision was the estimate of the extent to which the house would be damaged in an earthquake. The statement to which respondents reacted was: "If a major earthquake occurs, the damage to my house will (will not) be great, so insurance is (is not) a good buy." For nonpurchasers, this factor increased significantly as a justification for not buying insurance in three of the four counties; conversely, in Santa Clara County, this factor declined significantly in importance for insurance purchasers, although it was still of major importance (3.7 out of a possible 5.0).

Finally, there was little shift in the impact of expected state or federal grants or loans as a justification for either buying or forgoing insurance. The statement posed to the respondents was: "If a major earthquake occurs, the federal or state government will offer grants or loans that will (will not) be sufficient to rebuild my house." In all counties, this factor was more important in the decision for those who remained insured than those who remained uninsured: those who remained insured doubted that grants or loans would suffice, and therefore believed that it was important to purchase earthquake insurance. For those who were uninsured, this was not a particularly important factor in their decision. Only in Contra Costa County were there major shifts in the importance of this factor: here insurance purchasers found this factor to be less important in 1990 than in 1989, although in all counties and for all insurance purchase groups there was at least a moderately strong belief that such grants or loans would not be sufficient, necessitating private insurance.

Summary

A major theme of the analysis results of individual shifts before and after the Loma Prieta earthquake is the relative stability in both perception and behavior. The largest numbers of respondents who purchased insurance were concentrated in northern California, particularly in Santa Clara County. This finding suggests that direct experience with the earthquake induced insurance purchase, while indirect experience had little impact on either attitude or behavior.

Although the new purchasers also showed an attitude shift—they exhibited more concern for a future damaging earthquake—the remaining respondents showed stability in both attitude and behavior. Few of the respondents adopted new mitigation measures, whether insurance purchase or other investment, to safeguard their houses and contents.

The conclusion from this analysis of shift and stability is that direct experience with a major earthquake affected both attitudes and behavior whereas indirect experience had little impact on attitude or behavior toward earthquake damage mitigation. This finding suggests that general attitude toward earthquake vulnerability is the primary factor inducing insurance purchase and that direct experience with an earthquake provides an independent impetus to insurance purchase. In the next chapter, we will move from longitudinal analysis to a cross-sectional and spatial analysis of the impact of location with respect to earthquake damage on attitudes and behavior.

9
Locational Analysis

A number of questions about geographic location were included in the resurvey questionnaires sent to residents of Santa Clara and Contra Costa counties and in the supplemental survey questionnaire in Santa Clara County. Our geographic information system was used to determine the actual geographic location of each home and to measure the distance between the home and the active surface fault zones. Information received from the survey questions was used (1) to determine the relative geographic knowledge of the homeowners, (2) to study the relationship between damage experience and geographic location, and (3) to test for significant relationships between geographic location and adoption of earthquake insurance.

In this chapter, we will first examine the homeowners' general geographic knowledge and the importance they attached to geographic location as related to earthquake hazards. Next, we relate the homeowners' actual damage from the Loma Prieta earthquake to both actual and perceived distance to major faults. Finally, we examine the effects of geographic location (actual and perceived) and damage experience on perceived future earthquake hazards and adopted mitigation measures.

As the majority of earthquake related damage in our study counties occurred in Santa Clara County, this chapter primarily analyzes the responses from the homeowners there.

Location and Seismic Risk

The relationship between geographic location (e.g., magnitude of the earthquake, distance from fault breaks, local geologic conditions) and earthquake hazards was briefly discussed in chapter 2. We expected to find a relationship between distance from the 40 km fault break on the San Andreas

Table 30. Damaged homes in the supplemental survey and the resurvey

| | Amount of damage | | | | Total damage | |
| | $1-$1,000 | | > $1,000 | | | |
	#	%	#	%	#	%
Santa Clara	110	36.3	52	17.2	162	53.5
Contra Costa	23	7.8	7	2.4	30	10.2
Santa Clara supplemental	78	17.1	248	54.4	326	71.5
Expected damage	4	2.4	156	91.8	160	94.1
Spatially stratified	75	25.2	96	32.2	171	57.4

fault and patterns of earthquake-induced damage to the homes of survey respondents. Because the media directed considerable attention to geologic and topographic site conditions (e.g., the Bay Area mud under the collapsed apartment buildings), we expected respondents to be more aware of the characteristics of their home sites and the probable future stability of their homes in an earthquake. We also hypothesized that experience (either positive or negative) with the Loma Prieta earthquake would influence homeowners' beliefs that their homes were at greater or lesser risk to future earthquakes. We will begin the examination of these hypotheses by looking at actual patterns of earthquake damage and the cognitive maps of the homeowners.

Damage to Homes

The numbers and percentages of damaged homes in the resurvey of Santa Clara and Contra Costa counties and in the supplemental survey in Santa Clara County are shown in table 30. Only 11 percent of the respondents in Contra Costa County reported some damage to their houses or contents, whereas more than 53 percent of the homeowners in the resurvey of Santa Clara County experienced damage to their homes. About 17 percent of the Santa Clara resurvey respondents experienced more than $1,000 in damage. Because the new supplemental survey targeted homeowners whose property probably was damaged, more than 71 percent of this additional sample indicated some type of damage. The expected damage subset contained 156 respondents (91.8 percent) whose homes sustained more than $1,000 in damage.

The locations of the damaged homes in the Santa Clara County resurvey and the supplemental survey are shown in figures 11 and 12. As will be demonstrated, a significantly larger percentage of homes were damaged closer to the San Andreas fault zone than farther from this fault.

Geographic Knowledge

We conducted a number of analyses to determine the accuracy of the homeowners' geographic knowledge. We also studied homeowner percep-

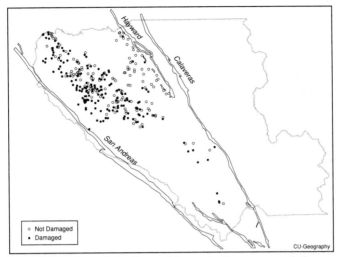

Fig. 11. Locations of the damaged homes in the resurvey of the respondents in Santa Clara County.

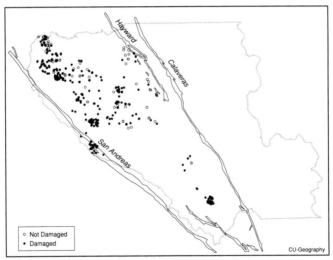

Fig. 12. Locations of the damaged homes in the supplemental survey of
the respondents in Santa Clara County.

tions of the relevant earthquake hazards: what factors were important to
them and how these factors might influence their mitigation activities. The
justification for investigating perceived risk as well as actual risk is the notion

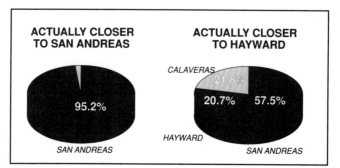

Fig. 13. Percentages of respondents indicating perceived closest fault to their homes.

of salience: if locational knowledge is important to people, they will act on the information they have regardless of its accuracy.

Nearby Faults

One of the simplest geographic questions we asked homeowners was the name of the active surface fault nearest their homes. We expected the respondents to name one of the three major active fault zones in the county—the San Andreas, Hayward, and Calaveras faults. In the 325 answers, 39 different active faults were named. Although the majority of answers (89 percent) gave one of the three major faults expected, several respondents named lesser known faults, and a few (6 percent) even wrote in a fictitious fault called "Loma Prieta."

To measure the accuracy of the actual nearest fault names, we compared the answers of only those respondents who named one of the three major faults (fig. 13). (Only nine homeowners actually lived closer to the Calaveras fault than the other major faults; the answers of these homeowners were not examined.) Almost all the homeowners closest to the San Andreas fault identified it as the closest. However, of the 87 homeowners who lived closer to the Hayward fault, fewer than 21 percent correctly identified it as the nearest fault (fig. 13). About 57 percent of the respondents living closer to the Hayward fault perceived the San Andreas fault as being closer. Undoubtedly, the San Andreas fault is a large presence in the minds of the Santa Clara residents.

Cognitive Distance from Faults

Several cartographic studies have examined from map-viewing experiments the relationship between cognitive distance and actual distance. People generally overestimate the length of straight lines on a map (Eboch 1983). In a study of an urban environment using an oral interview (without viewing a map), Lloyd and Heivly (1987) found that people tended to overestimate shorter distances between landmarks and underestimate longer distances. Some investigators have suggested that road systems and major topographical features can cause estimation errors (Canter and Tagg 1975). Other studies have shown that the nature of the landmark examined and its salience to the respondent can influence distance estimates (Sadalla and Staplin 1980).

Our study did not attempt to analyze the specific distance and directional distortions in cognitive maps. We hypothesized, however, that the cognitive distance to major active faults and their importance to homeowners would influence their beliefs about earthquake risks and subsequent mitigation activities.

The average distance between survey respondents' homes in Santa Clara County and one of the three major active fault zones is 4.9 miles. The average distance of all the homes in Santa Clara County to the San Andreas fault is only 8.0 miles. However, the average perceived distance to the nearest fault as reported by the homeowners in our study was 15.0 miles. A cumulative percentage curve of all respondents against increasing actual and perceived distance is shown in figure 14. The majority (77 percent) of the respondents in our study overestimated the distance to the nearest active surface fault. Despite this overestimation, there may still be a relationship between actual and perceived distance.

We used the Pearson and Spearman correlation statistics to measure the strength of a relationship between actual and perceived distance to the nearest active fault zone. A Spearman correlation measures the monotonic relation between two variables that are both measured on ordinal scales (Gravetter and Wallnau 1988).

The Pearson correlations between the actual and perceived distance to the nearest fault, and the actual and log of the perceived distance to the nearest fault were .12 and .28, respectively. The Spearman statistic for perceived distance was .26. (Note: The rank order of the logged values is the same as the raw perceived distances; thus, the Spearman values between actual distance and either the raw perceived or logged values are identical.) Thus, the linear relationship is weak at best.

We also examined the responses of only those homeowners who actually were closer to the San Andreas fault. To conduct this test we examined the responses of homeowners who indicated that the San Andreas Fault Zone was the nearest active fault to their home. Thus, the perceived distances between their home and the nearest active fault zone would also be the perceived distance between their home and the San Andreas fault zone. The results indicated a stronger linear relationship of .36 for the log of

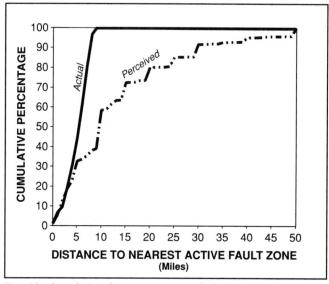

Fig. 14. Cumulative frequency curves of the actual and perceived distances between home locations and the nearest active surface fault.

perceived distance. The comparable Spearman test indicated a value of .33. The correlation tests indicated a statistically significant (at the .05 level) monotonic relationship between actual and perceived distances, although this relationship is very weak.

Perceived Effect of Location

We asked the homeowners in the resurvey and supplemental survey why they believed their homes were or were not damaged. We expected that the answers would be related to home location, house structure, or reasons admittedly unknown by the owner. We asked all homeowners the same general question and gave them choices of "proximity to fault/epicenter," "ground conditions," "house structure," "not sure," and a fill-in-the-blank option referred to as "other." For example, a respondent experiencing damage to the home might indicate, "My home was close to the fault/epicenter," whereas a homeowner not experiencing damage might indicate, "My home was not close to the fault/epicenter." In both cases, the answers indicated that the homeowners viewed distance to the fault/epicenter as an important reason for the damage or lack of damage to their homes. Not surprising, proximity to the fault/epicenter was indicated most frequently (42 percent) by the respondents, followed by ground conditions (26 percent) and house structure (25 percent). Only 19 percent of the respondents indicated that they were not sure why their houses were or were not damaged.

We expected that the reasons cited by those experiencing damage and those not experiencing damage would differ. The percentages of respondents indicating reasons for sustaining or not sustaining damage to their homes are illustrated in figure 15. Homeowners experiencing damage cited proximity (49 percent) most often, whereas they rarely cited ground conditions (4 percent) as the reason for their damage. In contrast, 54 percent of the respondents not experiencing damage gave "stable ground" as the main reason. Only 34 percent of the homeowners of undamaged homes believed them to be of sufficient distance from the San Andreas fault to not be damaged by Loma Prieta. Forty-six percent of the respondents whose homes did not receive damage believed that their house structures resisted earthquake damage.

Damage Experience and Geographic Knowledge

Home Damage and Locational Knowledge

The homes that experienced damage from the Loma Prieta earthquake were closer, on average, to the San Andreas fault zone than homes that were not damaged. The mean distances between the San Andreas fault for the damaged and undamaged homes differed for the two subsets: (1) all Santa Clara respondents and (2) those whose homes were closer to the San Andreas fault than to all other faults (table 31). The percentage of homes damaged by the Loma Prieta earthquake is graphed against the distance from the San Andreas fault in figure 16. These results clearly show that the attenuation of the shaking intensity decreases with increasing distance (although building

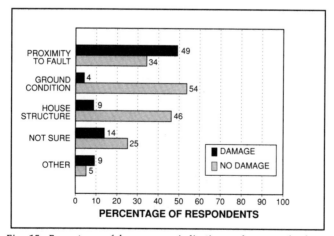

Fig. 15. Percentages of homeowners indicating each reason for homes experiencing or not experiencing damage. (Because some respondents indicated more than one reason, percentages total more than 100.)

Table 31. Distances (in miles) from the San Andreas fault zone and damage status in Santa Clara resurvey

	Damaged mean	Undamaged mean	t-probability
Actual distance			
To nearest fault	6.3	9.1	**.000**
Actually closer to San Andreas	5.0	6.1	**.000**
Perceived distance*			
To nearest fault	14.4	15.6	.085
Actually closer to San Andreas	13.3	15.3	**.005**

*The mean values shown are for actual reported perceived distances, but statistical tests used the log of the perceived distance.

structure and local site conditions undoubtedly modify shaking intensity and cause unstable sites).

Do the owners of the homes that experienced damage from the Loma Prieta earthquake perceive themselves as living closer to the San Andreas fault zone than owners of homes that were not damaged? To conduct this test we examined only the homeowners who indicated that the San Andreas fault zone was the nearest active fault to their homes. Thus, the perceived distances between their homes and the nearest active fault zone would also be the perceived distance between their homes and the San Andreas fault zone.

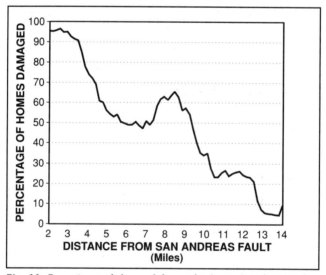

Fig. 16. Percentages of damaged homes by increasing distance from the San Andreas fault.

Table 32. Distances from the San Andreas fault zones and perceived earthquakes: Santa Clara resurvey

	Likely: Mean	Not likely: Mean	t-probability
Actual distance			
To nearest fault	4.8	5.2	.132
Actually closer to San Andreas	5.3	5.6	.149
Perceived distance*			
To nearest fault	14.3	15.9	.009
Actually closer to San Andreas	13.8	14.9	.011

*The mean values shown are for actual reported perceived distances, but statistical tests used the log of the perceived distance.

The results indicated that there is no significant relationship between perceived distance to the San Andreas fault and home damage (table 31). However, when examining only the homeowners who actually were closer to the San Andreas fault, we saw a very strong relationship between home damage and perceived distance to the fault.

Perceived Future Earthquakes and Distance

We found no relationship between actual distance to a fault and perceived vulnerability from future earthquakes (table 32). Respondents who considered an earthquake likely tended to have homes located at about the same distance from the San Andreas fault as those of respondents considering such an earthquake unlikely. The two groups were also located at about the same distance from the nearest fault, if it was other than the San Andreas.

However, a statistically significant relationship was found between perceived distance to the nearest active fault and estimated likelihood of a future earthquake damaging the respondent's home. Those who stated that they believed that a major damaging earthquake was likely tended to perceive themselves as located closer to the nearest fault or to the San Andreas fault. In sum, despite the fact that in reality their homes are no closer to the fault, homeowners who believe their homes are likely to be damaged in a future earthquake also perceive their homes as closer to active faults.

Insurance Adoption and Geographic Location

Our 1989 survey provided no evidence for adverse selection at the metropolitan level. However, considerable publicity in local newspapers followed the Loma Prieta earthquake, including published maps of geologic hazards and building damage. We expected this increase in information given to the residents of Santa Clara to result in a change in the adoption of earthquake insurance based on geographic location.

Table 33. Distances (in miles) from active fault zones and insurance status

	Insured: Mean	Uninsured: Mean	t-probability
1989 - BEFORE LOMA PRIETA			
To nearest fault			
Santa Clara	4.9	5.1	.597
Contra Costa	2.3	2.7	.204
Los Angeles	4.5	4.2	.485
San Bernardino	7.1	9.3	.179
To San Andreas			
Santa Clara	7.5	7.6	.648
San Bernardino	11.5	14.1	.094
Actually closer to San Andreas			
Santa Clara	5.3	5.6	.221
1990 - AFTER LOMA PRIETA			
To nearest fault			
Santa Clara	4.9	5.2	.175
Contra Costa	2.3	2.7	.056
Los Angeles	4.5	4.0	.254
San Bernardino	7.3	9.4	.218
To San Andreas			
Santa Clara	7.3	7.8	.233
San Bernardino	11.5	14.1	.096
Actually closer to San Andreas			
Santa Clara	5.2	5.7	.013

Note: Only those respondents who answered both the pre– and post–Loma Prieta surveys were included in this analysis.

Actual Distance between Insured and Uninsured

To test for adverse selection in the resurvey data, we used the Student's t-test to compare the mean distances between insured and uninsured homeowners and both the nearest active fault and the San Andreas fault. We found no evidence for the presence of adverse selection in any of the four counties using distance to the nearest fault or distance to the San Andreas fault (table 33).

However, when analyzing only the respondents who actually lived closer to the San Andreas fault than to other faults, we found a significant difference in the mean distances between the insured and uninsured groups (post–Loma Prieta insurance status) for Santa Clara County. This relationship is not significant for the same respondents when stratified by insurance status before Loma Prieta. Thus, the finding of significance may result from the change in spatial pattern caused by the respondents who purchased earth-quake insurance after Loma Prieta.

Distance and Three Groups of Insurance Status

We used a one-way analysis of variance to test for significant differences between the three groups of insurance status: never insured, insured before and after Loma Prieta, and newly insured after Loma Prieta. For the models that indicated a significant difference, we used separate t-tests to determine the two means that were significantly different.

No significant difference was found between the distances of the three groups of insurance status using distance to the nearest fault and distance to the San Andreas fault for all respondents in Santa Clara County (table 34). However, a statistically significant difference was found between the average distances of the two insured groups and the never insured group when analyzing only the homeowners who actually were closer to the San Andreas fault. Although the average distance (4.89 miles) to the fault of the newly insured homeowners was less than the distance (5.30 miles) of the group of homeowners insured before Loma Prieta, this difference was not statistically significant.

We used a similar set of tests to determine whether the perceived distances to the faults varied by insurance status group. We found a significant difference between the average distances of the two insured groups and the never insured group for distance to the nearest active fault and to the San Andreas fault. Here again no significant difference was found between the two groups of insured homeowners even though the newly insured homeowners, on average, were closer to the fault.

Table 34. Insurance status and distances (in miles) from active fault zones in the Santa Clara resurvey

	Newly insured: Mean	Remained insured: Mean	Never insured: Mean	F- probability
Actual distance				
To nearest fault	4.65	4.90	5.15	.381
To San Andreas	7.01	7.50	7.85	.415
Actually closer to S. Andreas	4.89	5.30	5.74	**.027**
Perceived distance*				
To nearest fault	10.35	13.61	17.97	**.002**
Actually closer to S. Andreas	10.06	11.16	18.62	**.005**

*The mean values shown are for actual reported perceived distances, but statistical tests used the log of the perceived distance.

These findings suggest that both groups of insured homeowners perceive themselves as closer to an active fault or the San Andreas fault than the
uninsured homeowners. Thus in the minds of the homeowners, adverse selection exists. For the county as a whole, adverse selection does not exist as
measured by distance to the nearest active fault. However, adverse selection
does exist after Loma Prieta for the homeowners closer to the San Andreas
fault than to any other fault. This perceived adverse selection may be a result
of the Loma Prieta earthquake.

Interaction between Damage and Insurance

Earlier in this chapter, we showed that on average the homes damaged
by Loma Prieta were closer to the San Andreas fault than were the undamaged homes. This finding, which is true regardless of insurance status, is
shown by using a t-test analysis of those respondents whose homes were
closer to the San Andreas fault than to other faults (table 35). Insured, damaged homes are closer to the San Andreas fault than uninsured, damaged
homes, using the post–Loma Prieta insurance status (table 36). Owners of insured, damaged homes also perceive themselves as closer to the San Andreas
fault than owners of uninsured, damaged homes (table 36). However, insurance status does not discriminate between the mean actual or perceived distance of the undamaged group. Thus, homeowner perception mirrors reality.
However, there is not a significant difference in the average perceived distance between the uninsured damaged and uninsured undamaged homes, as
there is in reality (table 35). This finding suggests that damage experience (or
lack of it) influenced the locational perception of the homeowners.

Table 35. Distances from San Andreas fault zone and damage status

	Damaged: Mean	Undamaged: Mean	t- probability
1989 - BEFORE LOMA PRIETA			
Actual distance			
Insured	4.84	6.38	.000
Uninsured	5.21	5.98	.004
1990 - AFTER LOMA PRIETA			
Actual distance			
Insured	4.77	6.23	.000
Uninsured	5.42	6.04	.031
Perceived distance*			
Insured	8.61	15.58	.001
Uninsured	19.99	15.37	.945

*The mean values shown are for actual reported perceived distance, but statistical tests used
the log of the perceived distance.

Table 36. Distances from San Andreas fault zone and insurance status

	Insured: Mean	Uninsured: Mean	t- probability
1989 - BEFORE LOMA PRIETA			
Actual distance			
Damaged	4.84	5.21	.209
Undamaged	6.38	5.98	.120
1990 - AFTER LOMA PRIETA			
Actual distance			
Damaged	4.77	5.42	**.028**
Undamaged	6.23	6.04	.445
Perceived distance*			
Damaged	8.61	19.99	**.001**
Undamaged	15.58	15.37	.937

*The mean values shown are for actual reported perceived distance, but statistical tests used the log of the perceived distance.

In summary, we found a significant relationship between actual distance and insurance status in the damaged subset with the post–Loma Prieta insurance status but not with the damaged subset using the pre–Loma Prieta insurance status. The homeowners (thirty-two in our sample) who were uninsured before Loma Prieta but are now insured generally experienced damage; twenty-one out of the thirty-one newly insured homeowners experienced damage. Thus it appears that the change in insurance status of these newly insured homeowners was enough to cause a significant difference in the analysis—adverse selection now exists.

Mandatory Earthquake Insurance

One earthquake insurance plan sponsored by the insurance industry includes a provision for mandatory earthquake insurance on all home loans guaranteed by the federal government. Earthquake and windstorm insurance are already mandatory in Puerto Rico. How do the homeowners in Santa Clara County feel about mandatory earthquake insurance? Are those homeowners who experienced damage from Loma Prieta more likely to accept the imposition of mandatory insurance? We included a question in our survey to address these questions. Only 20 percent of the respondents whose homes experienced $1,000 damage or less favored mandatory insurance (fig. 17). However, 42 percent of the homeowners whose homes experienced more than $1,000 damage from Loma Prieta agreed that earthquake insurance should be mandatory.

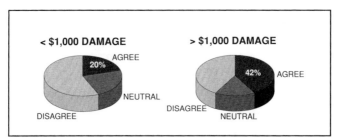

Fig. 17. *Attitudes toward mandatory earthquake insurance.*

Conclusions

Clearly, Santa Clara County residents are acutely aware of the hazard imposed on them by the San Andreas fault. This finding is indicated by their naming the San Andreas fault as the closest fault (even if it was not), the monotonic relationship between the actual distance to the San Andreas fault and perceived distance, and the respondents' rationale for experiencing or not experiencing damage to their own homes. However, they are not as acutely aware of the other major active faults and the risk associated with them, and they may be misled into thinking that the ground under their homes is stable and their houses are secure because their homes were not damaged—at least by the Loma Prieta earthquake.

The presence of adverse selection in the subgroup of homeowners who actually live closer to the San Andreas fault than other faults, coupled with the lack of adverse selection in the entire sample (measured by distance to the nearest fault), suggests that direct experience with Loma Prieta has resulted in adverse selection within Santa Clara county. Following the earthquake, homeowners have more information about the San Andreas fault (particularly geographic) on which to make decisions. The lack of adverse selection with all homeowners and their distance to the nearest fault suggests that the increase in geographic knowledge and behavioral changes are primarily associated with the San Andreas fault and not with other potentially dangerous faults. The presence of adverse selection (using either actual or perceived distance) indicates that experience with Loma Prieta has resulted in behavior changes primarily among those who experienced damage. Changes in attitudes and behavior are also evident in the widespread acceptance of the idea of mandatory insurance by those with considerable damage (greater than $1,000) to their homes and the less widespread acceptance by those whose homes were undamaged or had minimal damage.

10

The Effects of Experience: Implications for Policy and Further Investigation

Why do Californians purchase or refuse to purchase earthquake insurance? Does experience with an earthquake affect their behavior? What this study has tried to explore is the relationship between experience with an earthquake and changes in attitude and behavior.

This survey took advantage of the occurrence of an earthquake within a study area shortly after a previous study that assessed homeowner insurance purchase, adoption of other mitigation measures, and attitudes toward earthquake risk. Respondents in the four study counties were expected to change their responses to earthquakes in part depending on the intensity with which they experienced the 1989 Loma Prieta earthquake. The greatest shift in both attitude and behavior was expected to take place in the two northern California counties and especially in Santa Clara County, where the greatest damage occurred among the four study counties. In addition, those who suffered damage to their property or who lived near active faults were expected to have more intense reactions to the event.

Earthquake Experience and Changes in Attitudes and Behavior

The study has yielded four major findings that have implications for public policy. First, homeowners in all counties were generally more concerned with future earthquake risk after the Loma Prieta earthquake than they had been the year before. This effect, as expected, was slightly greater in the Bay Area counties than in the southern counties. Second, the purchase of earthquake insurance coverage increased in all four counties, but at a differential rate. Third, insurance purchasers tended to differ from nonpurchasers on the basis of percentage of the home value that was damaged in the earthquake, perceived vulnerability to future earthquakes, and value of their homes. Fourth, experience with the earthquake—as measured primarily by damage to one's own home and secondarily by geographic distance from the San Andreas fault—affected both perception of risk from future earthquakes and also perceived relative location. In this chapter, we will briefly review these principal findings and discuss their implications.

Increase in the Number of Policyholders

Previously, we had found that the percentages of households purchasing earthquake insurance coverage increased from 5 percent to up to 40 percent from 1973 to 1989. After the earthquake, there was a variable increase in the percentage of insured homeowners. However, the majority are still without earthquake coverage. Of the survey population, the percentage of homeowners with earthquake insurance ranges from a high of 51 percent in Santa Clara County to a low of 30 percent in Contra Costa County.

The survey county most impacted by the Loma Prieta earthquake, Santa Clara County, was also the place with the highest percentage increase in insurance purchase: almost 11 percent of the population purchased insurance within the twelve months after the Loma Prieta earthquake.

The primary reasons for not purchasing insurance after Loma Prieta were that it was too expensive or that the deductibles were too high. Fewer than 7 percent of the post–Loma Prieta uninsured said that earthquake insurance was not necessary, although almost 30 percent had given this response before Loma Prieta.

Although the numbers and percentages of policyholders have increased, the majority of California owner-occupiers are still uninsured against the earthquake peril, other than the mandatory $15,000 maximum coverage provided by the state. Almost 70 percent of Contra Costa County owner-occupiers do not have earthquake coverage, and even in Santa Clara County almost 49 percent remain uninsured against major losses.

General Increase in Concern about Future Earthquakes

Although increases in insurance purchase were modest, nonetheless there was a clear general increase in concern about a future earthquake. Respondents in all of the counties were more likely to believe that there was at least a one in ten chance of a strong earthquake of the size that struck San Francisco in 1906 occurring in their community in the next ten years. Similarly, there was a consistent increase in the belief that such an earthquake would cause at least 10 percent damage to one's own home in the next ten years. In Los Angeles County, 75 percent of the post–Loma Prieta respondents believed that their own homes would suffer such damage, up from 64 percent just a year before. Similar percentage increases were observed in the three other study counties as well.

These increased levels of concern occurred across insurance status. The new insurance purchasers tended to have greater increases in beliefs that, for example, there was at least a one in ten chance of an earthquake causing at least 10 percent damage to their homes in the next ten years. However, gains were also seen in all of the other insurance categories (the only exception was the nonpurchasers in Contra Costa County).

It is uncertain whether the Loma Prieta earthquake and the attendant publicity about earthquake hazards induced this increased concern. However, it is clear that eight to ten months after the earthquake, levels of concern remained elevated above those measured before the earthquake.

This increased concern did not translate itself into high rates of adoption of other mitigation measures. There has been a great deal of publicity about the kinds of measures households can take to protect their property from earthquake damage, and even more direct messages to households about the availability of earthquake insurance. That a moderate earthquake induces greater concern but relatively little change in behavior suggests that other factors causing resistance to behavior change may be at work.

Earlier in this book, we reviewed some of the factors that may impede the direct translation of concern with earthquake hazards into the purchase of insurance. Appropriate here is a selection of four such factors that have been suggested as impediments to the translation of knowledge into action (Palm 1990). These include: (1) a lack of resources, including intellectual skills, monetary resources, and time to consider and select the mitigation measure; (2) a belief that the individual cannot do anything in any case to prevent disaster; (3) use of a short-term rather than a long-term time frame in assessing individual susceptibility to the hazard and the appropriate response; and, most important, (4) the salience of the environmental hazard in comparison with other concerns in the daily life of the individual. In this survey, although we found that earthquake hazards had risen as a source of concern, we had no information on the relative salience of fear of earthquake-related damage as compared with personal or family problems, unemployment, crime, and so forth in the daily lives of the respondents.

New Insurance Purchasers vs. Nonpurchasers

A third major finding is that insurance purchasers tended to differ from nonpurchasers on several dimensions. Post–Loma Prieta earthquake insurance purchasers tended to have had damage to their homes in the earthquake, were located closer to the San Andreas fault, had higher perceptions of future risk from earthquakes, and had higher home values. However, as was found in the 1989 survey, socioeconomic and demographic variables did not distinguish the insured from the uninsured.

The 1989 survey found that while perceived future risk was an important discriminator between the insured and the uninsured, there was no consistent relationship between demographic and economic characteristics of the owner-occupiers and the propensity to purchase earthquake insurance. Thus, we would expect that while the post–Loma Prieta purchasers would have higher estimates of earthquake risk, a factor that might also be related to the extent to which their homes were damaged in the Loma Prieta earthquake, they would not differ in other demographic characteristics such as income or home value.

This study found that both home value (although not family income) and damage from the earthquake differentiated new purchasers from non-purchasers. Since the two surveys were conducted on the same sample, the difference between these two analyses suggests that the pre–Loma Prieta purchasers were not unlike the nonpurchasers in demographic and economic characteristics, while the post–Loma Prieta purchasers tended to have higher home values than the nonpurchasers (although similar incomes).

The results of this survey—and the finding of a distinct set of post-earthquake purchasers—suggest that the process of diffusion of earthquake insurance through the population of California residents may resemble more general diffusion processes. Although this study was not an empirical study of insurance adoption as an example of innovation diffusion, the parallels between the patterns we found and those suggested by diffusion theory suggest a possible rich vein of speculation. We will digress briefly to draw parallels between our empirical findings and the general diffusion principles.

Several authors (Gould 1969; Haggett, Cliff, and Frey 1977) have described the distribution of acceptors of innovation as a logistic curve or "S"-shaped cumulative proportion curve. In other words, after rapid initial adoption, the rate of adoption in a population slows until it reaches the maximum percentage who will adopt the innovation. Gould classified people into four types: innovators, the early majority, the later majority, and laggards based on when in the logistic process they adopted the innovation. After the innovation becomes accepted by a few, the early majority adopts the innovation at a rising rate. As the later majority adopts the innovation, the proportion of adoptions rises quickly, then slows, and then reaches a relatively steady state when only a small number of laggards continue to adopt the innovation. The spatial representation of the propagation of innovation waves has also been modeled (Hagerstrand 1952). In order to apply this type of model to the diffusion of earthquake insurance, more time-and-location series information about insurance adoption will be needed. However, the diverse work on spatial diffusion focusing on such examples as the acceptance of improved farm-

ing practices (Hagerstrand 1966), migration (Brown and Moore 1969), irrigation wells (Bowden 1965), urban ghettos (Morrill 1965), Rotary Clubs (Hagerstrand 1966), and cholera (Pyle 1969) suggests that this model might provide a
means to conceptualize the rate, path, and limit to the acceptance of earthquake insurance.

Earthquake insurance adoption may be a specific example of the more
general pattern of the diffusion of innovations. Whether the patterns and
processes that explain the spatial diffusion of innovations are applicable to
the adoption of earthquake insurance will await further study. However, if
insurance is such an example, it suggests that without further changes in the
inducements to purchase insurance voluntarily, some maxima of voluntary
insurance adoption could be projected. Indeed, this possibility is suggested by
Larry Brown's analysis of factors that lead to the establishment of innovation
diffusion: development of infrastructure, price, promotional communications, and market selection and segmentation (Brown 1980). He concluded
that price limits the "density of adoption" of an innovation, and therefore
influences the spatial distribution of innovation adoption. Further, "promotional communications"—the provision of information about the innovation to a selected part of the population—will also affect its ultimate distribution. These aspects of diffusion theory have direct implications for the study
of the adoption of earthquake insurance. Our empirical findings as well as
patterns suggested by diffusion theory give some indications that without
changes in the way insurance is sold or in the cost of insurance to the household, large percentages of California residents will continue to go uninsured
even in the aftermath of moderate-scale earthquakes.

Direct damage and proximity to active faults vs. risk perception

Homeowners in Santa Clara County have a general awareness of the
distance between their homes and the San Andreas fault. This awareness may
influence their attitudes toward their estimated vulnerability to a future
earthquake. Homeowners identified proximity to the fault break of the Loma
Prieta earthquake as a primary reason why their homes were damaged or not.
Homeowners who were uninsured before Loma Prieta but who purchased insurance after the earthquake were located closer to the San Andreas fault than
those who were still uninsured. These individuals also perceived that their
homes were located closer to the San Andreas fault. This fact suggests that the
subgroup of new purchasers is responding to their experience with damage.

Homeowners at comparable risk from other major active faults such as
the Hayward or Calaveras faults did not respond to the Loma Prieta earthquake with a similar shift in perceived vulnerability or the adoption of insurance. The apparent change in attitudes and behavior of the Santa Clara
County residents thus seems to reflect a response to a specific earthquake and

to estimates of a future earthquake associated with the San Andreas fault. Those at even greater risk of damage associated with other major faults did not share the same increase in levels of concern or in insurance adoption. This finding adds empirical evidence to the previous studies showing a linkage between experience and attitude formation. In this instance, experience with the Loma Prieta earthquake increased the salience and concreteness of the damage that can be associated with an earthquake.

Implications for Policy

Prospects for Further Increases in Insurance Coverage

The Loma Prieta earthquake was followed by a slight increase in insurance subscription, particularly in the areas most directly affected by the earthquake. The following year, in September 1990, state legislation was adopted that provides universal coverage for relatively small amounts of damage—up to $15,000 with a deductible of only $1000 for very low premiums. Although this legislation should cover a great deal of the damage to wood-frame, single-family dwellings in small-to-moderate earthquakes, it in no way replaces the need for coverage against catastrophic events. Indeed, in the moderate Loma Prieta earthquake, one-third (119) of the Santa Clara supplemental sample respondents had damage in excess of $10,000 and of those 50 had more than $100,000 in damage to their homes. Thus, catastrophic insurance is still needed.

The slight increase in the numbers of policyholders in spite of recent experience with an earthquake suggests that while mandated disclosure of earthquake risks and the availability of earthquake insurance as well as direct experience with a moderate earthquake can increase insurance subscription, there seems to be some limit on the percentage of the population that will be affected by these factors. If higher rates of voluntary private insurance subscription are a public policy goal, then attention should be given to clearer and more personalized risk messages and personalized offers of insurance, as well as regulation of premium rates. However, if wider coverage of the vulnerable population is intended, then clearly other measures must supplement the simple provision of information about risk and insurance availability. State or federal legislation that would provide subsidized earthquake insurance may, on the basis of these survey findings, be required in order to bring about substantial increases in earthquake insurance subscription.

Implications for Pending Federal Legislation

In the pre–Loma Prieta survey we found that most California owner-occupiers would be induced to purchase insurance if the deductibles and premiums were reduced. We expected that a moderate earthquake near a heavily populated area in combination with new predictions of increased probabilities of earthquake recurrence would result in large increases in insurance subscription.

The current survey continues to support the contention that a reduced premium rate would induce a vast majority of owner-occupiers to subscribe voluntarily. However, it is also clear that even experience with a moderate earthquake does not induce sufficient attitude change to result in major increases in insurance subscription. Voluntary insurance subscription, given the current rate structure, may have some natural limit and that limit may be reached shortly in California.

Implications of 1990 California Insurance Legislation

In October 1990, the governor of California signed into law a bill that would provide for the first mandatory earthquake insurance in the nation. The program will established a state reserve to insure homeowners against very small losses that otherwise would not be covered by the normal 10 percent deductible on standard policies (Roth 1990). The losses would be paid for through reserves provided by a small surcharge on residential insurance policies. The average charge was estimated at about $36 per year, depending on the local seismic risk and housing construction. Deductibles would normally be $1000, but could range up to $3500. Subscription to this program would be mandatory, and premiums would be collected by insurance companies as a surcharge on regular policies. The law went into effect for all residential insurance policies issued or renewed after July 1, 1991.

There is some question as to the "mandatory" nature of the new program. As was reported in March 1991 (*Natural Hazards Observer* 1991), "The California legislature did not specify a penalty or means of collection of unpaid surcharges, and the act contains no procedure to enforce its intent." They note that the Legislative Counsel of California stated that those who did not pay the surcharge would not be entitled to claims against the California Residential Earthquake Recovery Fund.

Since the program has not gone into effect at the time of this writing, it will be difficult to assess its impact. However, several outcomes are possible. First, the participation of homeowners in this new program may mean that interest in catastrophic earthquake insurance will also increase, serving to stimulate a new population of insurance purchasers. Since this type of state-administered program is relatively straightforward and inexpensive to implement, such a result would be a highly effective step toward the goal of universal insurance coverage.

On the other hand, the existence of the mandatory state program may convince owner-occupiers that it is not necessary to purchase insurance beyond the $15,000 provided by the state fund, and voluntary catastrophic earthquake insurance may decline. If households that drop coverage are also those at greatest risk from earthquake damage, this response would be very undesirable, since it would further increase vulnerability of a large part of the population to the impacts of a catastrophic earthquake.

The impacts of this new legislation on insurance purchase behavior will be very important and will bear careful scrutiny.

A Final Word

California still awaits its "great" earthquake—an earthquake that will have devastating impacts on life and property in one of the major metropolitan regions. California leads the nation in the measures it has adopted to increase the safety of its residents. Major efforts have resulted in strict building codes. A great deal of time and money has been invested in providing various forms of public information on earthquake hazards and methods that can be used to mitigate against damage. The state has mapped active surface fault rupture zones (Special Studies Zones), adopted strict building codes within these zones, and required the disclosure of these zones to prospective home buyers. The state has put in place an insurance plan that will provide small amounts of coverage—up to $15,000—as a bridge between the deductible and the regular coverage of an insurance policy. Finally, the state has mandated that insurance companies doing business in California offer earthquake insurance to all California customers.

Some California pundits have said that it takes an earthquake to induce California residents to pay attention to the earthquake hazard. In 1989 California experienced just such an earthquake. Yet a majority of our survey respondents continue to eschew investment in earthquake insurance or in any of the many measures they could adopt to reduce their vulnerability to earthquake-related damage.

What more can be done to increase voluntary mitigation? We must conclude that if portions of the population are found to be highly resistant to adopting voluntary mitigation measures, then mandatory measures that will decrease the vulnerability of these populations may be called for.

Appendix
Sample Questionnaire for Santa Clara County

INSTRUCTIONS:

Last spring, we sent a questionnaire to 3500 homeowners in Santa Clara, Contra Costa, Los Angeles, and San Bernardino Counties. You may have responded to our survey at that time.

This survey is a new set of questions that asks for your opinions on earthquake hazards and earthquake insurance as well as other information about your household. It should take you no more than 10 minutes to complete this form.

We thank you for your cooperation —your responses are very important.

Q-1   Please circle all that apply:

    YES   NO   Do you own the home listed at the address on the cover letter?

    YES   NO   Is this your primary residence?

IF YOU ANSWERED "NO" TO ANY OF THE ABOVE, PLEASE RETURN THIS FORM IN THE ENCLOSED STAMPED ENVELOPE. BY RETURNING THE QUESTIONNAIRE, WE WILL KNOW THAT WE SHOULD NOT CONTACT YOU AGAIN FOR THIS SURVEY. THANK YOU FOR YOUR HELP.

IF YOU ANSWERED "YES" TO ALL OF THE ABOVE, PLEASE CONTINUE ON TO QUESTION Q-2.

Q-2   Do you currently have earthquake insurance on this home? (Circle the number of your
       answer.)

       1   YES

                        | GO TO QUESTION Q-3. |

       2   NO

                  | GO TO QUESTION Q-7 ON PAGE 3. |

| PLEASE ANSWER THE FOLLOWING QUESTIONS ONLY IF YOU **DO HAVE**
EARTHQUAKE INSURANCE. |

Q-3   In what month and year did you get earthquake insurance on your present home?

       _____ (month) _____ (year)

Q-4   How much earthquake insurance coverage do you now have?

       $_____ (write in the dollar amount)

Q-5   How much does your earthquake insurance cost you each year?

       $_____ (cost)

Q-6   People take many things into account when they decide to buy earthquake insurance. On
       a scale from 1 to 5, with 1 being "not at all important" and 5 being "very important,"
       how did each of these affect your decision to buy insurance? (Circle the number from 1 to
       5 that best describes its importance.)

(a) I worry that an earthquake may destroy my home or cause major damage in the near future.

                    not at all important   very important
                         1   2   3   4   5
                         └____┴____┴____┴____┘

(b) Most of our family wealth is tied up in the equity of our house, which might be lost if an
     earthquake destroyed or damaged it.

                    not at all important   very important
                         1   2   3   4   5
                         └____┴____┴____┴____┘

(c)   The cost of insurance was acceptable to me.

not at all important   **very important**

1   2   3   4   5

(d)   I saw newspaper maps showing hazards areas, and decided that I needed earthquake insurance.

not at all important   **very important**

1   2   3   4   5

(e)   I watched a television program or read an article on earthquake hazards that convinced me that I needed to buy earthquake insurance.

not at all important   **very important**

1   2   3   4   5

(f)   If a major earthquake occurs, the damage to my house will be very great, so insurance is a good buy.

not at all important   **very important**

1   2   3   4   5

(g)   If a major earthquake occurs, the federal or state government will offer grants or loans that will not be sufficient to rebuild my house.

not at all important   **very important**

1   2   3   4   5

(h)   The October 1989 Loma Prieta earthquake in the San Francisco Bay Area made me more aware of the vulnerability of my house and its contents to damage, so insurance is a good buy.

not at all important   **very important**

1   2   3   4   5

(i)   Other (what?) _____.

not at all important   **very important**

1   2   3   4   5

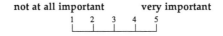

GO TO QUESTION Q-12 ON PAGE 5.

> **PLEASE ANSWER THE FOLLOWING QUESTIONS ONLY IF YOU <u>DO NOT HAVE</u> EARTHQUAKE INSURANCE.**

Q-7   People take many things into account when they decide **NOT** to buy earthquake insurance. On a scale from 1 to 5, with 1 being "not at all important" and 5 being "very important," how did each of these affect your decision **NOT** to buy insurance? (Circle the number from 1 to 5 that best describes its importance.)

(a)   I do not think that an earthquake may destroy my home or cause major damage in the near future.

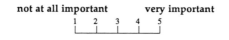

not at all important   very important
1   2   3   4   5

(b)   Not much of our family wealth is tied up in the equity of our house, and therefore we have little to lose if an earthquake destroyed or damaged it.

not at all important   very important
1   2   3   4   5

(c)   The cost of insurance was too high for me.

not at all important   very important
1   2   3   4   5

(d)   I saw newspaper maps showing hazards areas, and decided that I didn't need earthquake insurance.

not at all important   very important
1   2   3   4   5

(e)   I watched a television program or read an article on earthquake hazards that convinced me that I didn't need to buy earthquake insurance.

not at all important   very important
1   2   3   4   5

(f) If a major earthquake occurs, the damage to my house will be less than the deductible, so insurance is not a good buy.

not at all important   very important
1   2   3   4   5
|____|____|____|____|

(g) If a major earthquake occurs, the federal or state government will offer grants or loans that will be sufficient to rebuild my house, making insurance unnecessary.

not at all important   very important
1   2   3   4   5
|____|____|____|____|

(h) The October 1989 Loma Prieta earthquake in the San Francisco Bay Area made me more aware that my house and its contents are not vulnerable to damage, so insurance is not a good buy.

not at all important   very important
1   2   3   4   5
|____|____|____|____|

(i) Other (what?) _____ .

not at all important   very important
1   2   3   4   5
|____|____|____|____|

Q-8   Say you decided to buy earthquake insurance. How much coverage in dollars <u>would you want to have</u> on your house and its contents?

$_____ (total coverage)

Q-9   Most current policies have a 10% deductible, that is, you must pay for the first 10% of the value of the policy, and only after that will the insurance company pay for the additional damage. For example, if you had a $50,000 policy, you would pay for any damage up to $5,000. Given that fact, what would be the <u>highest</u> dollar amount that you would be willing to pay <u>each year</u> for that amount of coverage?

$_____ (cost)

Q-10 How much do you estimate it <u>currently</u> costs <u>each year</u> to have that much coverage?

$_____ (estimate of current cost)

Q-11   Have you ever tried to buy earthquake insurance for your house and/or its contents? (Circle the number of your answer.)

1   YES

If **YES**, what month and year was the last time you tried to buy earthquake insurance?

_____ (month) _____ (year)

Why didn't you buy earthquake insurance at that time? (Circle all that apply.)

1   It was not available.
2   It was too expensive.
3   The deductible was too high.
4   I decided I didn't need it.
5   Other (What?)_____.

2   NO, I have never tried to buy earthquake insurance.

PLEASE ANSWER THE FOLLOWING QUESTIONS <u>WHETHER OR NOT</u> YOU HAVE EARTHQUAKE INSURANCE.

Q-12   Some people have estimated the chances of a strong earthquake (of the size that struck San Francisco in 1906) happening in southern California in the next 10 years as 1 out of 5.

Now, please think about the chances of a 1906 San Francisco-type earthquake occurring <u>in your community.</u> What do you think are the chances that such an earthquake would occur in the next ten years in your community?

1 out of _____ (number)

Q-13   How likely do you think it is that <u>your own home</u> will be seriously damaged by an earthquake in the next ten years? (Circle the number of your answer.)

1   Very likely
2   Somewhat likely
3   Somewhat unlikely
4   Not very likely

Q-14   What are the chances of a 1906 San Francisco-type earthquake causing more than 10 percent damage to your own home in the next 10 years? One out of how many is your estimate of the chances of such an earthquake occurring in the next ten years?

1 out of _____ (number)

Q-15   Suppose a major damaging earthquake occurred in your community—of the magnitude of the 1906 San Francisco earthquake. How much damage (in dollars) would be caused to <u>the contents of your house as well as the house itself?</u>

$_____ (dollar value of damage to the house and contents)

Q-16   Please estimate how far you live from an active fault. _____
                                                                                                        (miles)

Q-17   Which active fault is closest to your home? _____
                                                                                                   (name of fault)

Q-18   How would you categorize the ground conditions on which your house is built with respect to earthquake risk? (Circle the number of your answer.)

1   LOW risk for earthquake damage
2   MODERATE risk for earthquake damage
3   HIGH risk for earthquake damage

THIS SECTION ADDRESSES THE OCTOBER 1989 LOMA PRIETA EARTHQUAKE IN THE SAN FRANCISCO BAY AREA, WHICH WAS THE MOST INTENSE EARTHQUAKE IN THAT AREA SINCE THE 1906 SAN FRANCISCO EARTHQUAKE.

Q-19   Was your house or its contents in any way damaged by the earthquake?

1   YES

GO TO QUESTION Q-20, NEXT PAGE

2   NO

If **NO**, why do you think your house <u>was not damaged</u>? (Circle all that apply.)

1   My house was not close to the fault/epicenter.
2   The ground conditions at my house are very stable.
3   My house structure resists earthquake damage.
4   Not sure why my house wasn't damaged.
5   Other _____ .

GO TO QUESTION Q-25, PAGE 8.

PLEASE ANSWER THE FOLLOWING QUESTIONS ONLY IF YOUR OWN HOUSE <u>WAS DAMAGED</u> IN THE OCTOBER 1989 LOMA PRIETA EARTHQUAKE THAT OCCURRED IN THE SAN FRANCISCO BAY AREA.

Q-20   On a scale from 1 to 5, please indicate how serious the damage was to your house and contents.

not seriously   very seriously
damaged   damaged

1   2   3   4   5

Q-21   Please estimate the total amount of damage to your house and its contents in dollars.

$_____ (total damage)

Q-22   Why do you think your house <u>was damaged</u>? (Circle all that apply.)

1   My house was close to the fault/epicenter.
2   The ground conditions at my house are unstable.
3   My house structure was not adequate for this type of earthquake.
4   Not sure why my house was damaged.
5   Other _____.

Q-23   Was any of the damage covered by federal or state aid? (Circle the number of your answer.)

1   YES
        If **YES**, how much of the damage was paid for in federal or state aid?
        $_____ (total payment received)
2   NO
3   DON'T KNOW

Q-24   Was any of this damage covered by insurance? (Circle the number of your answer.)

1   YES
        If **YES**, how much of the damage was paid for in insurance claims?
        $_____ (total payment received)
2   NO
3   DON'T KNOW

PLEASE ANSWER THE FOLLOWING QUESTIONS <u>**WHETHER OR NOT**</u> YOUR HOUSE WAS DAMAGED IN THE OCTOBER 1989 LOMA PRIETA EARTHQUAKE WHICH OCCURRED IN THE SAN FRANCISCO BAY AREA.

Q-25   About how far from your house was the nearest house **seriously** damaged (that is, over $5,000 in damage) by the Loma Prieta earthquake? (Circle the number of your answer.)

1   Within 1 block
2   1 to 2 blocks away
3   3 to 5 blocks away
4   6 to 10 blocks away
5   More than 10 blocks away

Q-26   Do you personally know anyone who was injured in the earthquake? (Circle the number
of your answer.)

1   YES
2   NO
3   DON'T KNOW

Q-27   Did you have any family or friends whose houses were damaged in the earthquake?
(Circle the number of your answer.)

1   YES
2   NO
3   DON'T KNOW

Q-28   Was your travel inconvenienced by this earthquake? For instance, traffic was heavier
on the highways, bridges were closed, etc. (Circle the number of your answer.)

not at all			very	
inconvenienced			inconvenienced	
1	2	3	4	5

Q-29   In what other ways was your normal routine disrupted? (Please describe.)

_____
_____
_____
_____
_____
_____

Q-30   **Since the October 1989 Loma Prieta earthquake in the San Francisco Bay Area,** have
you done anything to minimize the amount of damage an earthquake might cause to
your home?

1   YES
If **YES**, what did you do?   Month/ Year   Cost

_____
_____

2   NO
If **NO**, why haven't you taken steps to protect your home? (Circle one or more
numbers.)

1   Too expensive
2   Won't help
3   Insurance will cover costs
4   Never got around to it
5   Don't have the time
6   Other (what?)_____

Q-31   What is your opinion of the following statement?
"Everyone in California should be required to purchase some earthquake insurance."
(Circle the number of your answer.)

Q-32   Do you believe earthquake insurance should be sold by: (Place a check by your answer.)

Private industry	_____ YES	_____ NO
State government	_____ YES	_____ NO
Federal government	_____ YES	_____ NO

THANK YOU FOR YOUR PARTICIPATION IN THIS SURVEY.

References

Algermissen, S. T., E. P. Arnold, K. V. Steinbrugge, S. L. Hanson, and M. G. Hopper. 1990. *Probabilistic and Scenario Estimates of Losses to Dwellings in California.* U.S. Geological Survey Open File Report 90-323.

Algermissen, S. T., J. C. Stepp, W. A. Rinehart, and E. P. Arnold. 1969. *Studies in Seismicity and Earthquake Damage Statistics.* Department of Commerce, Report (Appendix B) COM-71-00053. Washington, DC: Department of Commerce.

Anderson, Dan, and Maurice Weinrobe. 1981. *Geographic Mortgage Risk: Implications for the Federal Home Loan Mortgage Corporation.* Washington, DC: Kaplan, Smith.

Arrow, Kenneth J. 1970. "The Theory of Risk Aversion." In *Essays in the Theory of Risk-Bearing,* edited by K. J. Arrow, 90-109. New York: North-Holland.

Averill, J. R. 1987. "The Role of Emotions and Psychological Defense in Self-Protective Behavior." In *Taking Care: Understanding and Encouraging Self-Protective Behavior,* edited by N. D. Weinstein, 54-78. New York: Cambridge University Press.

Babcock, Henry. 1968. *Appraisal Principles and Procedures.* Homewood, IL: Irwin.

Bay Area Regional Earthquake Preparedness Project (BAREPP). 1990. "Loma Prieta and Its Lessons." *Networks Earthquake Preparedness News* 5(1): 2-6.

Berry, Brian J. L. 1976. "Ghetto Expansion and Single-Family Housing Prices: Chicago, 1968-72." *Journal of Urban Economics* 3:397-423.

Beshers, James M. 1962. *Urban Social Structure.* New York: Free Press.

Blalock, Hubert M. 1979. *Social Statistics.* New York: McGraw-Hill.

Blankenship, Frank J. 1986. *The Prentice-Hall Real Estate Appraisal Deskbook.* Englewood Cliffs, NJ: Prentice-Hall.

Bloom, George F., and Henry S. Harrison. 1978. *Appraising the Single Family Residence.* Chicago: American Institute of Real Estate Appraisers.

Bowden, Leonard. 1965. *Diffusion of the Decision to Irrigate.* University of Chicago, Department of Geography, Research Paper no. 97. Chicago: University of Chicago Department of Geography.

Brown, James. 1987. "Using the Insurance and Finance Industries to Influence Purchase of Earthquake Insurance: Antitrust Considerations." Paper presented to a workshop sponsored by

George Washington University under contract with the Federal Emergency Management Agency, Boulder, CO, July 17-18.

Brown, James M., and Peter Gerhart. 1989. *Utilization of the Mortgage Finance and Insurance Industries to Induce the Private Procurement of Earthquake Insurance: Possible Antitrust Implications.* University of Colorado, Institute of Behavioral Science, Working Paper no. 66. Boulder: University of Colorado.

Brown, Lawrence A. 1980. *Studies in the Diffusion of Innovation.* Ohio State University, Department of Geography, Discussion Paper no. 60. Columbus: Ohio State University.

Brown, Lawrence A., and Eric G. Moore. 1969. "Diffusion Research: A Perspective." In *Progress in Geography*, edited by C. Board, R. J. Chorley, Peter Haggett, and D. R. Stoddart, 120-57. London: Edward Arnold.

Burby, Raymond J., Scott A. Bollens, James M. Holloway, Edward Kaiser, David Mullan, and John R. Sheaffer. 1988. *Cities under Water.* University of Colorado, Institute of Behavioral Science, Program in Environment and Behavior, Monograph no. 47. Boulder: University of Colorado.

Burton, Ian, and Robert W. Kates. 1964. "The Perception of Natural Hazards in Resource Management." *Natural Resources Journal* 3:412-41.

Camerer, Colin, and Howard Kunreuther. 1989. "Experimental Markets for Insurance." *Journal of Risk and Uncertainty* 2:265-300.

Canter, D., and S. Tagg. 1975. "Distance Estimation in Cities." *Environment and Behavior* 7:59-80.

Chaiken, Shelly, and Charles Stangor. 1987. "Attitudes and Attitude Change." *Annual Review of Psychology* 38:575-630.

Combs, B., and Paul Slovic. 1979. "Newspaper Coverage of Causes of Death." *Journalism Quarterly* 56:837-43.

Cross, John. 1985. "Resident's Acceptance of Hurricane Hazard Mitigation Measures: Final Summary Report." Mimeo.

Dames and Moore. 1990. "Loss-Reduction Provisions of a Federal Earthquake Insurance Program." In *Hearings before the Subcommittee on Policy Research and Insurance of the Committee on Banking, Finance, and Urban Affairs, House of Representatives, serial no. 101-168*, pp. 294-515.

Dillman, Don. 1978. *Mail and Telephone Surveys: The Total Design Method.* New York: Wiley.

Doyle, James K., Gary H. McClelland, William D. Schulze, Steven R. Elliott, and Glenn W. Russell. 1991. "Protective Responses to Household Risk: A Case Study of Radon Mitigation." *Risk Analysis* 11:121-34.

Drabek, Thomas E. 1986. *Human System Responses to Disaster: An Inventory of Sociological Findings.* New York: Springer-Verlag.

Earthquake Project of the National Committee on Property Insurance. 1989. *Catastrophic Earthquakes: The Need to Insure against Economic Disaster.* Boston: National Committee on Property Insurance.

Eboch, M. 1983. "The Cartographic Scale: A Cognitive Investigation." Master's thesis, University of South Carolina.

Edwards, W. 1955. "The Prediction of Decisions among Bets." *Journal of Experimental Psychology* 50:201-14.

Einhorn, Hillel, and Robin Hogarth. 1985. "Ambiguity and Uncertainty in Probabilistic Inference." *Psychological Review* 92:433-61.

Ellsberg, Daniel. 1961. "Risk, Ambiguity, and the Svage Axioms." *Quarterly Journal of Economics* 75:643-69.

Evernden, J. F., and J. M. Thomson. 1985. "Predicting Seismic Intensities." In *Evaluating Earthquake Hazards in the Los Angeles Region: An Earth-Science Perspective,* edited by J. I. Ziony, 151-202. U.S. Geological Survey Professional Paper 1360. Reston, VA: U.S. Geological Survey.

Fazio, R. H., J. Chen, E. C. McDonel, and S. J. Sherman. 1982. "Attitude Accessibility, Attitude-Behavior Consistency, and the Strength of Object-Evaluation Association." *Journal of Experimental Social Psychology* 18:339-357.

Fazio, R. H., and M. P. Zanna. 1978. "Attitudinal Qualities Relating to the Strength of the Attitude-Behavior Relationship." *Journal of Experimental Social Psychology* 14:398-408.

Fazio, R. H., M. P. Zanna, and J. Cooper. 1978. "Direct Experience and Attitude Behavior Consistency: An Information Processing Analysis." *Personality and Social Psychology Bulletin* 4:48-51.

Federal Home Loan Bank Board. 1988. *Savings and Home Financing Source Book: Annual.* Washington, DC: Office of Thrift Supervisor.

Gould, Peter R. 1969. *Spatial Diffusion.* Association of American Geographers, Commission on College Geography, Resource Paper no. 4. Washington, DC: Association of American Geographers.

Gravetter, F. J., and L. B. Wallnau. 1988. *Statistics for the Behavioral Sciences.* 2d ed. New York: West Publishing.

Greene, Marjorie, Ronald Perry, and Michael Lindell. 1981. "The March 1980 Eruptions of Mt. St. Helens: Citizen Perceptions of Volcano Threat." *Disasters* 5(1): 49-66.

Hagerstrand, Torsten. 1952. *The Propagation of Innovation Waves.* Lund Studies in Geography, series B, no. 4, pp. 3-19. Lund: Gleerup.

_____. 1966. "Aspects of the Spatial Structure of Social Communication and the Diffusion of Information." *Papers of the Regional Science Association,* no. 16, pp. 27-42.

Haggett, Peter, Andrew D. Cliff, and A. E. Frey. 1977. *Locational Analysis in Human Geography.* 2d ed. London: Edward Arnold.

Hart, Earl W. 1985. *Fault-Rupture Hazard Zones in California.* Sacramento: Department of Conservation, Division of Mines and Geology.

Hodge, David, Virginia Sharp, and Marion Marts. 1979. "Contemporary Responses to Volcanism: Case Studies from the Cascades and Hawaii." In *Volcanic Activity and Human Ecology,* edited by Payson D. Sheets and Donald K. Grayson, 221-48. New York: Academic Press.

Hogarth, Robin M., and Howard Kunreuther. 1989. "Risk, Ambiguity and Insurance." *Journal of Risk and Uncertainty* 2:5-35.

Janis, I. L. 1967. "Effect of Fear Arousal on Attitude Change: Recent Developments in Theory and Experimental Research. In *Advances in Experimental Social Psychology,* edited by L. Berkowitz, 4:166-224. New York: Academic Press.

Janoff-Budman, R. 1985. "Criminal vs. Noncriminal Victimization: Victims' Reactions." *Victimology* 10:498-511.

Johnston, R. J. 1978. "Land Values, Housing Prices, and Housing Shortages: A Geographical Perspective." In *An Invitation to Geography,* edited by David A. Lanegran and Risa Palm, 175-88. 2d ed. New York: McGraw-Hill.

Kahneman, D., and Amos Tversky. 1979. "Prospect Theory: An Analysis of Decision under Risk." *Econometrica* 47(2): 263-91.

Kates, Robert W. 1971. "Natural Hazard in Human Ecological Perspective: Hypotheses and Models." *Economic Geography* 47:438-51.

Keeney, Ralph L., and Detlof von Winterfeldt. 1986. "Improving Risk Communication." *Risk Analysis* 6(4): 417-24.

Kunreuther, Howard. 1990. "Testimony of Howard C. Kunreuther before the Subcommittee on Policy Research and Insurance of the House Committee on Banking, Finance, and Urban Affairs." In *Hearings before the Subcommittee on Policy Research and Insurance of the Committee on Banking, Finance, and Urban Affairs, House of Representatives, serial no. 101-168*, pp. 762-93. Washington, DC: U.S. Government Printing Office.

Kunreuther, H., R. Ginsberg, L. Miller, P. Sagi, P. Slovic, B. Borkan, and N. Katz. 1978. *Disaster Insurance Protection: Public Policy Lessons.* New York: Wiley.

Kunreuther, Howard, and Anne E. Kleffner. 1991. "Should Earthquake Mitigation Measures Be Voluntary or Required?" Wharton School, University of Pennsylvania, Risk and Decision Process Center, Working Paper no. 91-04-01.

Kwiatkowski, Dennis. 1990. "Statement of the Federal Emergency Management Agency." In *Hearings before the Subcommittee on Policy Research and Insurance of the Committee on Banking, Finance, and Urban Affairs, House of Representatives, serial no. 101-168*, pp 97-114. Washington, DC: U.S. Government Printing Office.

Laska, Shirley B. 1986. "Involving Homeowners in Flood Mitigation." *Journal of the American Planning Association* 52(4): 452-66.

Lichtenstein, Sara, Paul Slovic, Baruch Fischoff, M. Layman, and B. Combs. 1978. "Judged Frequency of Lethal Events." *Journal of Experimental Psychology: Human Learning and Memory* 4:551-78.

Lloyd, R., and C. Heivly. 1987. "Systematic Distortions in Urban Cognitive Maps." *Annals of the Association of American Geographers* 72:532-48.

McNutt, Stephen R. 1990. "Summary of Damage and Losses Caused by the Loma Prieta Earthquake." In *The Loma Prieta (Santa Cruz Mountains), California, Earthquake of 17 October 1989*, pp. 131-38. California Department of Conservation, Division of Mines and Geology, Special Publication 104. Sacramento: California Department of Conservation.

McNutt, Stephen R., and Tousson R. Toppozada. 1990. "Seismological Aspects of the 17 October 1989 Earthquake." In *The Loma Prieta (Santa Cruz Mountains), California, Earthquake of 17 October 1989*, pp. 11-27. California Department of Conservation, Division of Mines and Geology, Special Publication 104. Sacramento: California Department of Conservation.

Marcuse, Peter. 1990. "United States of America." In *International Handbook of Housing Policies and Practices,* edited by Willem van Vliet, 327-76. New York: Greenwood.

Mattingly, Shirley. 1988. "Response and Recovery Planning with Consideration of the Scenario Earthquakes Developed by California Division of Mines and Geology." In *Proceedings of Conference 41: A Review of Earthquake Research Applications in the National Earthquake Hazards Reduction Program: 1977-1987,* edited by Walter W. Hays, 550-54. U.S. Geological Survey, Open File Report 88-13-A. Reston, VA: U.S. Geological Survey.

Mileti, Dennis S., Barbara C. Farhar, and Colleen Fitzpatrick. 1990. *Risk Communication and Public Response to the Parkfield Earthquake Prediction Experiment.* Report to the National Science Foundation. Fort Collins: Colorado State University Hazards Assessment Laboratory and Department of Sociology.

Montz, B. E. 1982. "The Effect of Location on the Adoption of Hazard Mitigation Measures." *Professional Geographer* 34(4): 416-23.

Morrill, Richard. 1965. "The Negro Ghetto: Problems and Alternatives." *Geographical Review* 55:339-361.

Mulilis, John-Paul, and Richard Lippa. 1990. "Behavioral Change in Earthquake Preparedness Due to Negative Threat Appeals: A Test of Protection Motivation." *Journal of Applied Social Psychology* 20:619-38.

Natural Hazards Observer. 1991. "Mandatory Earthquake Insurance Not So Mandatory." *Natural Hazards Observer* 15 (March): 6.

Nisbett, R. E., and L. Ross. 1980. *Human Inference: Strategies and Shortcomings.* Englewood Cliffs, NJ: Prentice-Hall.

Noll, Roger G., and James E. Krier. 1990. "Some Implications of Cognitive Psychology for Risk Regulation." *Journal of Legal Studies* 19:747-79.

Palm, Risa. 1979. "Financial and Real Estate Institutions in the Housing Market: A Study of Recent House Price Changes in the San Francisco Bay Area." In *Geography and the Urban Environment*, edited by D. T. Herbert and R. J. Johnston, 2:83-123. Chichester: John Wiley.

_____. 1981a. *The Geography of American Cities.* New York: Oxford University Press.

_____. 1981b. *Real Estate Agents and Special Studies Zones Disclosure: The Response of California Home Buyers to Earthquake Hazards Information.* Institute of Behavioral Science, Program on Technology, Environment and Man, Monograph no. 32. Boulder: University of Colorado.

_____. 1990. *Natural Hazards: An Integrative Framework for Research and Planning.* Baltimore: Johns Hopkins University Press.

Palm, Risa, Michael Hodgson, Denise Blanchard, and Donald Lyons. 1990. *Earthquake Insurance in California: Environmental Policy and Individual Decision-Making.* Boulder: Westview Press.

Palm, Risa, with Sallie Marston, Patricia Kellner, David Smith, and Maureen Budetti. 1983. *The Response of Lenders and Appraisers to Earthquake Hazards.* University of Colorado at Boulder, Institute of Behavioral Science, Monograph no. 38. Boulder: University of Colorado.

Perloff, L. S. 1983. "Perceptions of Vulnerability to Victimization." *Journal of Social Issues* 39: 41-61.

Perrin, Constance. 1977. *Everything in Its Place: Social Order and Land Use in America.* Princeton, NJ: Princeton University Press.

Petty, R. C., and J. T. Cacioppo. 1986. "The Elaboration Likelihood Model of Persuasion." *Advanced Experimental Social Psychology* 19:123-205.

Pyle, Gerald F. 1969. "Diffusion of Cholera in the United States." *Geographical Analysis* 1:59-75.

Ratcliff, Richard U. 1965. *Modern Real Estate Valuation: Theory and Applications.* Madison, WI: Democrat Press.

Roder, Wolf. 1961. "Attitudes and Knowledge on the Topeka Flood Plain." In *Papers on Flood Problems*, edited by G. F. White. Chicago: University of Chicago, Department of Geography, Research Paper no. 70. Chicago: University of Chicago Department of Geography.

Rossi, Peter H., James D. Wright, Eleanor Weber-Burdin, and Joseph Pereira. 1983. *Victims of the Environment: Loss from Natural Hazards in the United States, 1970-1980.* New York: Plenum.

Roth, Richard. 1990. "The New California Residential Earthquake Recovery Fund and the Need for a Federal Earthquake Recovery Program." In *Hearings before the Subcommittee on Policy Research and Insurance of the Committee on Banking, Finance, and Urban Affairs, House of Representatives, serial no. 101-168*, pp. 830-36. Washington, DC: Government Printing Office.

Ruckelshaus, W. D. 1983. "Science Risk and Public Policy." *Science* 221:1026-28.

Saarinen, Thomas. 1982. *Perspectives on Increasing Hazard Awareness*. University of Colorado, Institute of Behavioral Science, Program on Environment and Behavior, Monograph no. 35. Boulder: University of Colorado.

Sadalla, E., and L. Staplin. 1980. "The Perception of Traversed Distance." *Environment and Behavior* 12:65-79.

Schiff, Myra. 1977. "Hazard Adjustment, Locus of Control, and Sensation Seeking: Some Null Findings." *Environment and Behavior* 9:233-54.

Schoemaker, Paul. 1987. "Preferences for Information on Probabilities versus Prizes: Tests of Expected Utility Type Models." University of Chicago, Center for Decision Research, Working Paper.

Simpson-Housley, Paul, and Peter Bradshaw. 1978. "Personality and the Perception of Earthquake Hazard." *Australian Geographical Studies* 16:65-72.

Slovic, Paul. 1986. "Informing and Educating the Public about Risk." *Risk Analysis* 6(4): 403-15.

Slovic, Paul, Howard Kunreuther, and Gilbert F. White. 1974. "Decision Processes, Rationality, and Adjustment to Natural Hazards." In *Natural Hazards: Local, National, and Global,* edited by G. F. White. New York: Oxford University Press.

Steinbrugge, Karl V. 1990. "Earthquake Losses to 1-to-4-Family California Dwellings: Who Pays." In *Hearings before the Subcommittee on Policy Research and Insurance of the Committee on Banking, Finance, and Urban Affairs, House of Representatives, serial no. 101-168,* pp. 798-814. Washington, DC: Government Printing Office.

Steinbrugge, Karl V., and S. T. Algermissen. 1990. *Earthquake Losses to Single-Family Dwellings: California Experience.* U.S. Geological Survey Bulletin 1939. Washington DC: Government Printing Office.

Steinbrugge, K. V., F. E. McClure, and A. J. Snow. 1969. *Studies in Seismicity and Earthquake Damage Statistics.* Department of Commerce, Report (Appendix A) COM-71-00053. Washington, DC: Department of Commerce.

Stewart Economics. 1989. "The Economic Impact of a Major Earthquake." In *Catastrophic Earthquakes: The Need to Insure against Economic Disaster,* Appendix D. Boston: National Committee on Property Insurance.

Thier, Herbert D. 1988. "The California Earthquake Education Program." In *Proceedings of Conference 41: A Review of Earthquake Research Applications in the National Earthquake Hazards Reduction Program: 1977-1987,* edited by Walter W. Hays, 65-74. U.S. Geological Survey, Open File Report 88-13-A. Reston, VA: U.S. Geological Survey.

Time Magazine. 1982. "Califoreclosure: Creative Financing's Dark Side." *Time* 119 (June 14): 65.

Turner, Ralph H., Joanne Nigg, Denise Heller Paz, and Barbara Shaw Young. 1979. *Earthquake Threat: The Human Response in Southern California.* Los Angeles: University of California–Los Angeles, Institute for Social Science Research.

———. 1980. *Community Response to Earthquake Threat in Southern California: Part Five Action Response in the Public.* Los Angeles: University of California–Los Angeles, Institute for Social Science Research.

Tversky, Amos, and D. Kahneman. 1981. "The Framing of Decisions and the Psychology of Choice." *Science* 211:453-58.

Weinstein, N. D. 1987. "Unrealistic Optimism about Illness Susceptibility: Conclusions from a Community-Wide Sample." *Journal of Behavioral Medicine* 10:481-500.

———. 1989a. "Effects of Personal Experience on Self-Protective Behavior." *Psychological Bulletin* 105:31-50.

———. 1989b. "Optimistic Biases about Personal Risks." *Science* 246:1232-33.

White, Gilbert F., and J. Eugene Haas. 1975. *Assessment of Research on Natural Hazards.* Cambridge: Massachusetts Institute of Technology Press.

Willinger, Marc. 1989. "Risk Aversion and the Value of Information." *Journal of Risk and Insurance* 56:320-28.

Index

THE UNIVERSITY OF CHICAGO
GEOGRAPHY RESEARCH PAPERS
(Lithographed, 6 x 9 inches)

Titles in Print

165. JONES, DONALD W. *Migration and Urban Unemployment in Dualistic Economic Development.* 1975. x + 174 p.

166. BEDNARZ, ROBERT S. *The Effect of Air Pollution on Property Value in Chicago.* 1975. viii + 111 p.

167. HANNEMANN, MANFRED. *The Diffusion of the Reformation in Southwestern Germany, 1518-1534.* 1975. ix + 235 p.

168. SUBLETT, MICHAEL D. *Farmers on the Road: Interfarm Migration and the Farming of Noncontiguous Lands in Three Midwestern Townships. 1939-1969.* 1975. xiii + 214 p.

169. STETZER, DONALD FOSTER. *Special Districts in Cook County: Toward a Geography of Local Government.* 1975. xi + 177 p.

172. COHEN, YEHOSHUA S., and BRIAN J. L. BERRY. *Spatial Components of Manufacturing Change.* 1975. vi + 262 p.

173. HAYES, CHARLES R. *The Dispersed City: The Case of Piedmont, North Carolina.* 1976. ix + 157 p.

174. CARGO, DOUGLAS B. *Solid Wastes: Factors Influencing Generation Rates.* 1977. 100 p.

176. MORGAN, DAVID J. *Patterns of Population Distribution: A Residential Preference Model and Its Dynamic.* 1978. xiii + 200 p.

177. STOKES, HOUSTON H.; DONALD W. JONES; and HUGH M. NEUBURGER. *Unemployment and Adjustment in the Labor Market: A Comparison between the Regional and National Responses.* 1975. ix + 125 p.

180. CARR, CLAUDIA J. *Pastoralism in Crisis. The Dasanetch and Their Ethiopian Lands.* 1977. xx + 319 p.

181. GOODWIN, GARY C. *Cherokees in Transition: A Study of Changing Culture and Environment Prior to 1775.* 1977. ix + 207 p.

183. HAIGH, MARTIN J. *The Evolution of Slopes on Artificial Landforms, Blaenavon, U.K.* 1978. xiv + 293 p.

184. FINK, L. DEE. *Listening to the Learner: An Exploratory Study of Personal Meaning in College Geography Courses.* 1977. ix + 186 p.

185. HELGREN, DAVID M. *Rivers of Diamonds: An Alluvial History of the Lower Vaal Basin, South Africa.* 1979. xix + 389 p.

186. BUTZER, KARL W., ed. *Dimensions of Human Geography: Essays on Some Familiar and Neglected Themes.* 1978. vii + 190 p.

187. MITSUHASHI, SETSUKO. *Japanese Commodity Flows.* 1978. x + 172 p.

188. CARIS, SUSAN L. *Community Attitudes toward Pollution.* 1978. xii + 211 p.

189. REES, PHILIP M. *Residential Patterns in American Cities: 1960.* 1979. xvi + 405 p.

190. KANNE, EDWARD A. *Fresh Food for Nicosia.* 1979. x + 106 p.

192. KIRCHNER, JOHN A. *Sugar and Seasonal Labor Migration: The Case of Tucumán, Argentina.* 1980. xii + 174 p.

194. HARRIS, CHAUNCY D. *Annotated World List of Selected Current Geographical Serials, Fourth Edition. 1980.* 1980. iv + 165 p.

196. LEUNG, CHI-KEUNG, and NORTON S. GINSBURG, eds. *China: Urbanizations and National Development.* 1980. ix + 283 p.

197. DAICHES, SOL. *People in Distress: A Geographical Perspective on Psychological Well-being.* 1981. xiv + 199 p.

198. JOHNSON, JOSEPH T. *Location and Trade Theory: Industrial Location, Comparative Advantage, and the Geographic Pattern of Production in the United States.* 1981. xi + 107 p.

199-200. STEVENSON, ARTHUR J. *The New York–Newark Air Freight System.* 1982. xvi + 440 p.

201. LICATE, JACK A. *Creation of a Mexican Landscape: Territorial Organization and Settlement in the Eastern Puebla Basin, 1520-1605.* 1981. x + 143 p.

202. RUDZITIS, GUNDARS. *Residential Location Determinants of the Older Population.* 1982. x + 117 p.

204. DAHMANN, DONALD C. *Locals and Cosmopolitans: Patterns of Spatial Mobility during the Transition from Youth to Early Adulthood.* 1982. xiii + 146 p.

206. HARRIS, CHAUNCY D. *Bibliography of Geography. Part II: Regional. Volume 1. The United States of America.* 1984. viii + 178 p.

.207-208. WHEATLEY, PAUL. *Nagara and Commandery: Origins of the Southeast Asian Urban Traditions.* 1983. xv + 472 p.

209. SAARINEN, THOMAS F.; DAVID SEAMON; and JAMES L. SELL, eds. *Environmental Perception and Behavior: An Inventory and Prospect.* 1984. x + 263 p.

210. WESCOAT, JAMES L., JR. *Integrated Water Development: Water Use and Conservation Practice in Western Colorado.* 1984. xi + 239 p.

211. DEMKO, GEORGE J., and ROLAND J. FUCHS, eds. *Geographical Studies on the Soviet Union: Essays in Honor of Chauncy D. Harris.* 1984. vii + 294 p.

212. HOLMES, ROLAND C. *Irrigation in Southern Peru: The Chili Basin.* 1986. ix + 199 p.

213. EDMONDS, RICHARD LOUIS. *Northern Frontiers of Qing China and Tokugawa Japan: A Comparative Study of Frontier Policy.* 1985. xi + 209 p.

214. FREEMAN, DONALD B., and GLEN B. NORCLIFFE. *Rural Enterprise in Kenya: Development and Spatial Organization of the Nonfarm Sector.* 1985. xiv + 180 p.

215. COHEN, YEHOSHUA S., and AMNON SHINAR. *Neighborhoods and Friendship Networks: A Study of Three Residential Neighborhoods in Jerusalem.* 1985. ix + 137 p.

216. OBERMEYER, NANCY J. *Bureaucrats, Clients, and Geography: The Bailly Nuclear Power Plant Battle in Northern Indiana.* 1989. x + 135 p.

217-218. CONZEN, MICHAEL P., ed. *World Patterns of Modern Urban Change: Essays in Honor of Chauncy D. Harris.* 1986. x + 479 p.

219. KOMOGUCHI, YOSHIMI. *Agricultural Systems in the Tamil Nadu: A Case Study of Peruvalanallur Village.* 1986. xvi + 175 p.

220. GINSBURG, NORTON; JAMES OSBORN; and GRANT BLANK. *Geographic Perspectives on the Wealth of Nations.* 1986. ix + 133 p.

221. BAYLSON, JOSHUA C. *Territorial Allocation by Imperial Rivalry: The Human Legacy in the Near East.* 1987. xi + 138 p.

222. DORN, MARILYN APRIL. *The Administrative Partitioning of Costa Rica: Politics and Planners in the 1970s.* 1989. xi + 126 p.

223. ASTROTH, JOSEPH H., JR. *Understanding Peasant Agriculture: An Integrated Land-Use Model for the Punjab.* 1990. xiii + 173 p.

224. PLATT, RUTHERFORD H.; SHEILA G. PELCZARSKI; and BARBARA K. BURBANK, eds. *Cities on the Beach: Management Issues of Developed Coastal Barriers.* 1987. vii + 324 p.

225. LATZ, GIL. *Agricultural Development in Japan: The Land Improvement District in Concept and Practice.* 1989. viii + 135 p.

226. GRITZNER, JEFFREY A. *The West African Sahel: Human Agency and Environmental Change.* 1988. xii + 170 p.

227. MURPHY, ALEXANDER B. *The Regional Dynamics of Language Differentiation in Belgium: A Study in Cultural-Political Geography.* 1988. xiii + 249 p.

228-229. BISHOP, BARRY C. *Karnali under Stress: Livelihood Strategies and Seasonal Rhythms in a Changing Nepal Himalaya.* 1990. xviii + 460 p.

230. MUELLER-WILLE, CHRISTOPHER. *Natural Landscape Amenities and Suburban Growth: Metropolitan Chicago, 1970-1980.* 1990. xi + 153 p.

231. WILKINSON, M. JUSTIN. *Paleoenvironments in the Namib Desert: The Lower Tumas Basin in the Late Cenozoic.* 1990. xv + 196 p.

232. DUBOIS, RANDOM. *Soil Erosion in a Coastal River Basin: A Case Study from the Philippines.* 1990. xii + 138 p.

233. PALM, RISA, AND MICHAEL E. HODGSON. *After a California Earthquake: Attitude and Behavior Change.* 1992. xii + 130 p.